Web Design

PEARSON

Harlow, England • Lon...   ...land • Singapore • Hong Kong
Tokyo • Seoul • Taipei   ...erdam • Munich • Paris • Milan

Pearson Education Limited

Edinburgh Gate
Harlow CM20 2JE
Tel: +44 (0)1279 623623
Fax: +44 (0)1279 431059
Website: www.pearson.com/uk

First edition published in 2010
Second edition published in Great Britain in 2012

© Joe Kraynak and James A. Brannan 2010, 2012

The rights of Joe Kraynak and James A. Brannan to be identified as authors of this work have been
asserted by them in accordance with the Copyright, Designs and Patents Act 1988.

Pearson Education is not responsible for the content of third-party internet sites.

ISBN: 978-0-273-77472-3

British Library Cataloguing-in-Publication Data
A catalogue record for this book is available from the British Library

Library of Congress Cataloging-in-Publication Data
A catalog record for this book is available from the Library of Congress

10 9 8 7 6 5 4 3 2 1
16 15 14 13 12

Typeset in 11/14 pt ITC Stone Sans by 3
Printed and bound in Great Britain by Scotprint, Haddington

Web Design

in Simple steps

Second Edition
Joe Kraynak and
James A. Brannan

Use your computer with confidence

Get to grips with pratical computing tasks with minimal time, fuss and bother.

In Simple Steps guides guarantee immediate results. They tell you everything you need to know on a specific application; from the most essential task to master, to every activity you'll want to accomplish, through to solving the most common problems you'll encounter.

Helpful features:

To build your confidence and help you get the most out of your computer, practical hints, tips and shortcuts feature on every page:

ALERT: Explains and provides practical solutions to the most commonly encountered problems

HOT TIP: Time and effort saving shortcuts

SEE ALSO: Points you to other related tasks and information

DID YOU KNOW? Additional features to explore

WHAT DOES THIS MEAN?
Jargon and technical terms explained in plain English

Practical. Simple. Fast.

in **Simple** steps

Dedication:

For Lee Borup and Weber State University's Veterans Upward Bound (VUB) Project. A chance encounter opened an entirely new world. Had we never met, I would never have acquired an education or written this book.

Author acknowledgements:

Thanks to the staff at Pearson, especially Rob Cottee and Steve Temblett. Also thanks to Neil Salkind. Thanks to the many sites that graciously allowed me to use screenshots from their sites. Special thanks to Everaldo and his open source Crystal Project icons, www.everaldo.com; these icons are beautiful and make my books much nicer.

Publisher's acknowledgements:

We are grateful to the following for permission to reproduce copyright material:

Screenshots on pp.2, 4, 7, 8, 9, 17, 23, 27, 29, 31, 34, 35, 36, 37, 45, 46, 49, 53, 55, 56, 59, 64, 65, 66, 76, 81, 86, 87, 88, 91, 93, 94, 98, 99, 100, 101, 105, 108, 118, 119, 120, 124, 125, 145, 146, 150, 157, 158, 162, 164, 165, 167, 192, 194 courtesy of James A. Brannan Associates PLLC; screenshots on pp.3, 15, 41, 77, 176 from FreeCSStemplates.org; screenshots on pp.6, 8, 15, 43, 52, 80, 184 from Directgov © Crown copyright; screenshots on pp.11, 162, 168, 172, 173, 185, 187 courtesy of Google, Inc; screenshots on pp.15, 137 from Flickr, reproduced with permission of Yahoo! Inc © 2012 Yahoo! Inc. YAHOO!, the YAHOO! Logo, FLICKR and the FLICKR logo are registered trademarks of Yahoo! Inc; screenshot on p.18 from Oxfam International, reproduced with permission of Oxfam GB, www.oxfam.org.uk. Oxfam GB does not necessarily endorse any text or activities that accompany the materials; screenshots on pp.26, 54, 78 from Animenation; screenshots on p.40 from the Food Standards Agency; screenshot on p.48 from www.cultuer. gov.uk, Department for Culture, Media and Sport (dcms) © Crown Copyright; screenshot on p.51 from NHSDirectWales © Crown copyright; screenshot on p.60 from British Sky Broadcasting Limited; screenshot on p.60 courtesy of JavaWorld; screenshot on p.60 courtesy of Studio B Productions Inc.; screenshots on p.73 © WWF-UK; screenshots on p.79 from the Campaign Against Euro-Federalism; screenshots on p.80 from The Department of Health © Crown copyright; screenshot on p.83 from SurvivalInternational.org; screenshots on pp.95, 96, 139, 141, 142, 178, 182, 192 from Adobe Systems, Inc; screenshot on p.110 courtesy of Xara Group Ltd.; screenshot on p.136 from iStockphoto, Getty Images; screenshots on pp.171, 186 from SeoQuake, courtesy of SeoQuake Team and SEMrush.com; screenshot on p. 83 design an coding by Nomensa, content by Broads Authority; screenshot on p.84 from MadebySplendid.com; screenshots on pp.163, 189 from FinkShrink.com; screenshots on pp.193, 194 from Bluehost.

In some instances we have been unable to trace the owners of copyright material, and we would appreciate any information that would enable us to do so.

in Simple steps

Contents at a glance

Contents

2 Website architecture

3 Writing your text

Top 10 Web Design Problems Solved

Top 10 Web Design Tips

Tip 1: Use a content management system (CMS)

Web design tends to focus on the front end, the appearance of the site. However, the back end is also important. You want to design a site that is easy to configure and easy to post content to and edit. A content management system (CMS), such as WordPress, Joomla or Drupal, simplifies the tasks of designing and maintaining a website.

1 Notice that when you log into a CMS, it provides tools for posting content to the site, choosing a design template and configuring the site in other ways.

2 Post content as easily as you create and save a document in a word processing application.

3 Open a page or blog post, edit it and click a button to update it. Editing is that easy!

You can easily install WordPress, Joomla or Drupal from the control panel that most web hosting services provide. These popular CMSs are well supported, so many free and premium themes are available for them. In addition, because so many developers use them, help is available for most of the problems you are likely to encounter.

HOT TIP: You can use WordPress and most other CMSs to create a static website, a blog or a combination website/blog. You can set up users to have several people contribute content to the site, which is often essential in a business or organisation.

Tip 2: Provide a service

This tip runs a close second to the number one tip. As you will see, throughout this book I repeat the mantra 'users come to your site to fulfil a need, not to bask in your design brilliance'. You fulfil needs by providing a service. If you remember nothing else from the book, remember this tip.

1 This book's entire premise is related to this tip, particularly Chapter 1. When finished with the book, review the websites mentioned throughout and think about the services each one provides.

2 Follow the steps presented in Chapter 1 to try to determine the services your site might provide – before you start analysis and design!

3 If interested in learning more, navigate to Wikipedia and look up Web 2.0, which is strongly focused on offering services to users.

Tip 3: Do not get too clever

Clever web design is usually not usable web design. Nobody cares about your website's cleverness except perhaps other web designers and web design, coffee-table books. When I get clever with web design the results are usually disastrous.

1 Review the Flash site templates throughout this book. Without exception, they are brilliant but not very usable for a typical website.

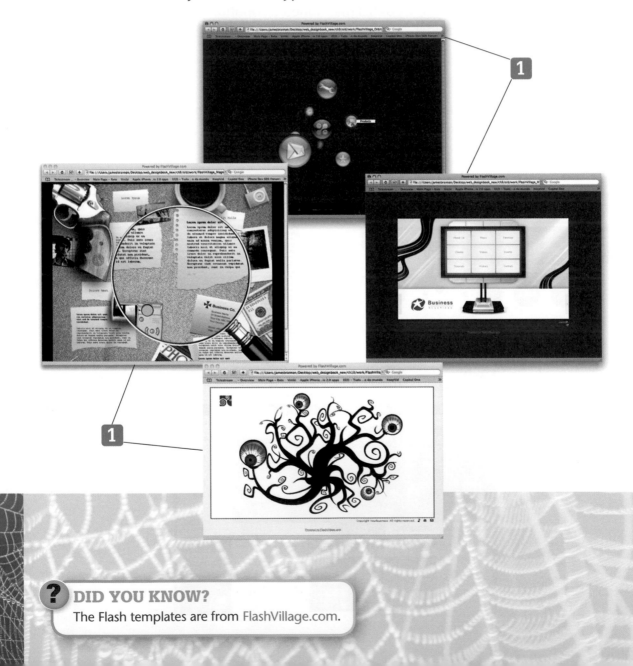

2 Here's a preview of several of my clever hypothetical webpages presented throughout this book. I think I am being clever, but in reality I am simply making the pages less usable.

HOT TIP: Avoid eye candy. Eye candy consists of elements such as JavaScript clocks, menus with special effects and other assorted nonfunctional additions to your website.

Tip 4: Usability is paramount

This tip is actually many combined into one. Remember, usability is paramount. If a user cannot use your site, he or she will leave it. These steps, previewed here, are discussed in more detail later in this book.

1. Remember to use relative sizes for fonts, not fixed-size fonts.

2. Use a liquid layout to accommodate browser size variation.

3. Ensure visited links are a different colour from non-visited links.

4. Be certain images enhance your site's message and are not mere decorations.

5. Ensure users can scan your webpages by using headings and chunking your information.

6. Ensure your site is accessible for users with disabilities by including features such as alt tags for images.

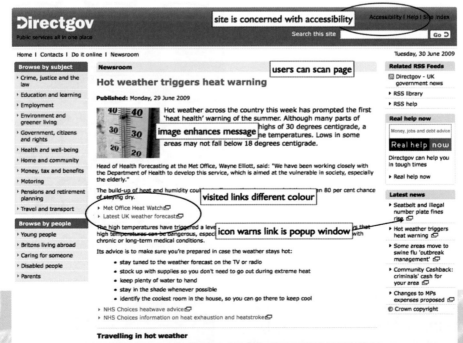

Tip 5: The Web is an easily changeable medium

When faced with all the steps presented in this book, do not get overwhelmed. Webpages, unlike traditional software, are easily updatable. You can publish your webpages before being complete and you can easily update them once published. So don't be afraid to make mistakes, they are easily corrected.

1 Realise this tip is not advocating 'under construction' pages (see Chapter 2), but rather is simply reminding you that a website does not require being 100 per cent complete before being published. The example below shows a tutorial website released before finishing tutorials.

2 It is often said that the final 10 per cent of a software project usually accounts for 90 per cent of the effort. If you wait until your site is 100 per cent complete, then there is a probability it will never be published. Once you publish your site, you have a greater incentive to finish it, particularly if you start getting positive feedback from users.

Tip 6: Make text more accessible with plenty of headings, subheadings and lists

You will find this tip expanded upon in Chapter 3 of this book. You should use short information chunks, write like a journalist and use ample headings, subheadings and lists. Journalists present the most important information at a story's beginning. Headings and subheadings help users ascertain a paragraph's topic without actually reading the chapter. All of these tips help 'skim-reading' users determine your webpage's content without actually having to read the entire page in detail.

1. Navigate to the Directgov website (www.direct.gov.uk). Navigate to one of the numerous articles on the site.

2. Notice that the page shown here provides information for Britons who will be living abroad.

3. Notice the page has ample headings and subheadings.

4. The page presents the information in small information chunks that are easy to read.

5. The page also provides links to more detailed information should a user desire more information on a topic.

6. Notice that without reading the page you can ascertain that it contains information on moving to the European Union and taxes, pensions and benefits when abroad. You gain all this information by merely scanning the headers.

Directgov
Public services all in one place

Cymraeg | Accessibility | Help | Site index | A A A

Search this site _____ Go

Home | Contacts | Do it online | Newsroom | Video   Friday, 24 February 2012

Browse by subject
- Crime and justice
- Education and learning
- Employment
- Environment and greener living
- Government, citizens and rights
- Health and well-being
- Home and community
- Money, tax and benefits
- Motoring
- Pensions and retirement planning
- Travel and transport

Browse by people
- Young people
- **Britons living abroad**
- Caring for someone
- Disabled people
- Parents

Britons living abroad

Britons living abroad

▶ **Before you go**
- Preparing to move or retire abroad
- Cultural awareness
- Travel and keep safe when living abroad
- Exporting your vehicle (motoring section)
- More about before you go

▶ **Money abroad**
- Benefits
- National Insurance
- Pensions
- More about money

▶ **Education and jobs while abroad**
- Children and schools
- Voluntary work abroad
- Working abroad
- Studying at an overseas university
- Teaching English as a Foreign Language (TEFL)

▶ **Health abroad**
- Travel insurance (travel and transport section)
- European Health Insurance Card (travel and transport section)

ⓘ **See also...**
- Passports and visas (travel and transport section)
- Emergencies abroad (travel and transport section)
- Voting from abroad (government, citizens and rights section)
- Tax on rental income (money, tax and benefits section)

Bookmark with:
Facebook | Twitter | StumbleUpon | Delicious | Reddit
▶ How do you use this toolbar?

Domestic violence - get help

Don't suffer in silence. Find out about the advice, help and support that's available to you
▶ Domestic violence: protecting yourself and getting help

Retiring abroad

▶ Visit pensions, benefits and tax when retiring abroad

Do it online
▶ Apply online to replace your driving licence
▶ Find schools and Sure Start Children's Centres
▶ Find a job now
▶ Exchanging your foreign driving licence

Tip 7: Check your work

You should always test your site. A site with spelling mistakes and incorrect grammar is not a convincing site. Check your site's grammar and spelling. A site with broken hyperlinks, missing images and other mistakes also results in an unprofessional site.

1. Check your site's appearance, spelling, grammar and links using more than one browser.

2. Solicit feedback from test users to assess your site's usability.

3. Make sure your site is accessible to all users regardless of their abilities or disabilities.

4. Test your site's speed and compare it to competing websites.

5. Audit your site for search engine optimisation.

6. Validate your site's HTML and CSS source code to eliminate errors and ensure compliance with web standards.

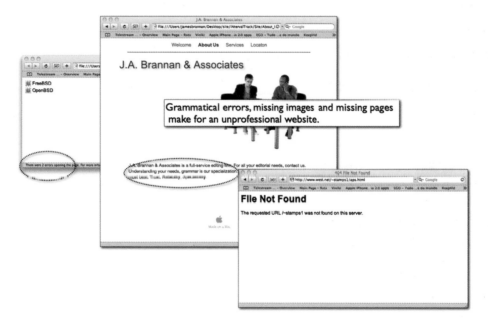

Grammatical errors, missing images and missing pages make for an unprofessional website.

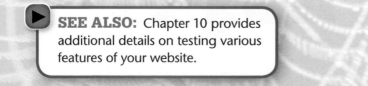

SEE ALSO: Chapter 10 provides additional details on testing various features of your website.

Tip 8: Be consistent

Consistency is as important as having a well thought out, accurate site. Maintain the same look, feel and navigation throughout the site. This tip will become more apparent as you progress through the book.

1 Use a consistent background or header to give your site a sense of unity as users skip from page to page.

2 Build consistent navigation into your site, so users always know where to click to access what they want.

Tip 9: Leverage the power of free online web developer tools

The Web is packed with free tools for web developers. You can find free CMSs including WordPress and Drupal, Google Webmaster Tools and Analytics and a host of addons and extensions for web browsers that can help you troubleshoot problems with HTML and CSS, test your site's speed, audit search engine optimisation (SEO) and much more. In addition, developers are very generous in helping one another solve problems they encounter. Take full advantage of these free tools and information.

1 Use developer tools for web browsers to assist in website analysis, troubleshooting and development.

2 Search for online tools to test site speed, SEO, HTML and CSS validation and more.

3 Seek help online for specific problems you encounter and for advice on how to produce specific design features.

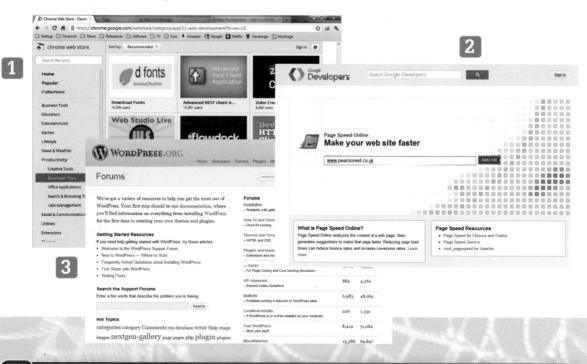

HOT TIP: Many valuable tools are available for specific CMSs, such as WordPress. You can install plugins that improve site security, increase performance, improve search engine optimisation, incorporate social sharing buttons, add an email contact form to your site and just about anything else you need or can imagine.

Tip 10: Remember, web design is supposed to be fun

Web design is challenging, but it should also be a fun and exciting endeavour. Designing a site that is attractive, functional and popular is like throwing a party and seeing that all your guests are having the time of their lives. Having fun is an essential component of creativity.

1 When web developers enjoy building websites it shows in their work.

2 If you enjoy web design, then consider pursuing it as a career. Web design does not require a computer science degree, nor does it require an art degree, although any formal training you can obtain is certainly of value.

1 Planning your website

Introduction

Before developing a site, you should plan. Plan what you wish to accomplish through the website. After knowing what you or your client wishes to accomplish, you then brainstorm what service you might offer a user. A successful site offers services to its users.

Review several sites' services and self-interested goals

Providing services to a user population brings the desired users to your site and keeps them coming back. But you must also have a clear understanding of your goals and tailor the services your site offers so it fulfils your goals.

1 Navigate to each site listed in Table 1.1 on page 16 and review each one.

2 Notice the service each site offers.

3 Now notice the self-interested goals each site fulfils for its owners.

HOT TIP: Review competitors' websites. Assess what they did poorly and what they did well. Avoid your competitors' mistakes and emulate their achievements.

Table 1.1 Services offered by several sites and how the services meet the owner's goals

Site	Service offered	Self-interest goals
www.freecss templates.org	Offers free CSS templates.	Provides a link to paid templates and sells advertising. Provides a creative outlet for template author's energy.
www.bodybuilding.com	Provides an extensive exercise database. Provides thousands of training articles. Provides an extensive user forum to share information on exercise topics.	Has positioned itself as the leading online retailer to buy nutrition supplements.
www.google.com	Provides the best search engine on the Internet.	Sells advertising.
www.flickr.com	Provides a central location where photographers can share their art.	Sells advertising. Allows users to upgrade to paid membership for premium services.
www.iratblu.blogspot.com	Provides a blog where readers can waste time and vicariously read about someone else's life. Allows a user to post opinions to her posts.	Enables author to explore her creative side and to log and share her thoughts and experiences with a personal and international audience.
www.michaelmcintyre.co.uk	Provides fans with news, information, tour dates, video clips of performances and access to merchandise related to their favourite comedian.	Personal branding site provides comedian with an online presence and a way to grow his fan base online.
www.direct.gov.uk	Provides a central information clearinghouse on everything related to the UK government.	Provides the public with self-serve access to government information and services, thus relieving some of the burden of providing information and services.
www.bikeman.com	Features new product announcements and reviews by bicycle and outdoor enthusiasts for bicycle and outdoor enthusiasts. Also offers instructions on common bicycle repairs.	Enables Bikeman to establish itself as a leading online retailer of bicycles, accessories, clothing and other related products.

Determine your site's purpose

After deciding to build a website, the first thing you should do is determine the site's purpose. What are its goals? What are your goals? Do the site's goals and your goals complement each other? Are the goals the same?

1 Determine your goals (or your client's goals). For instance, suppose you are developing the product shown here.

2 Write the goals down, in order, and refine the list. These are the goals for a website I wish to develop to promote my hypothetical product and my writing.

> **! ALERT:** The goals are your goals. The goals are not hypothetical user goals, those goals come later. You need to be clear about what you want your site to do for you.

> **Site goals:**
>
> 1. Give away freeware product on the internet.
>
> 2. Promote programming abilities.
>
> 3. Obtain new consulting business.
>
> 4. Promote books.
>
> 5. Obtain new book contracts.

> **! ALERT:** Be careful you do not get analysis paralysis. Do not try defining too many goals in too much detail. Keep it high level. Try limiting your goals to 10 at most.

> **🔥 HOT TIP:** Do not assume you already know your goals. I am an automaton, I often do things without knowing why, and chances are you do too.

Narrow your purpose to one goal

Although this step might seem superficial, it helps you focus on your single most important goal. You should have a single, clear goal before design.

1 Condense your goals into one main goal.

2 Consider whether the goal is sufficiently concrete and at the right level. For instance, if your goal is 'to create a personal webpage', you gain little insight into your true goal as this goal is too wide-ranging. Cut through the rhetoric and find the true goal.

3 Navigate to www.oxfam.org.uk and notice the site's goal. 'Oxfam is a global movement of people working with others to overcome poverty and suffering.' The site (and the organisation) has one goal: to overcome poverty and suffering in the world.

HOT TIP: Make the website's goal sufficiently detailed so that it has a clear meaning and purpose.

Identify your target audience

Every website has a target audience. Some sites have a narrow audience while others have a wider one. Understand the different visitors you wish to attract to your site.

Some questions for considering a site's potential audience include the following:

- How many different visitor types (groups) will the site attract?
- What are each group's characteristics?
- Are there any potential roadblocks that prevent reaching your goals with a particular group? For instance, is your product too expensive? Is a large group segment visually impaired? Is a group's primary language not English?
- Why should each group visit your site?
- What are each group's favourite sites?
- How different or similar is each group?
- Do you need to narrow your appeal to fewer groups?

1 Consider your site's primary users.

2 Consider other users that might visit your site.

3 Remember, all this book's remaining chapters must be considered in light of your target audience.

4 Consider the FirstNews (www.firstnews.co.uk) website's target users are children, so the site's design reflects this audience.

5 Broaden your consideration to other, less important users than your primary user.

6 The FirstNews website's secondary users are teachers and parents. Although consistent in appearance, the teachers' area is designed to appeal more to teachers and parents.

! ALERT: All sites have a 'casual user', the casual surfer who stumbles upon your site. Always ask yourself how important this user is. Remember, you can't please everyone all the time.

4

6

Have a call to action

Brian and Jeffrey Eisenberg wrote a book entitled *Call to Action: Secret Formulas to Improve Online Success*. In it, they discuss having a call to action. Key to any site's success is persuasion. If your site persuades a user to do what you wish them to do, then your site is a success. Key to persuasion is having a call to action.

1 Navigate to the National Trust's website (www.nationaltrust.org.uk).

2 Note that the site prominently displays several calls to action: Find a place to visit, Join, Donate, Volunteer.

3 Notice the site also contains an option to shop and an opportunity to bid at a charity auction.

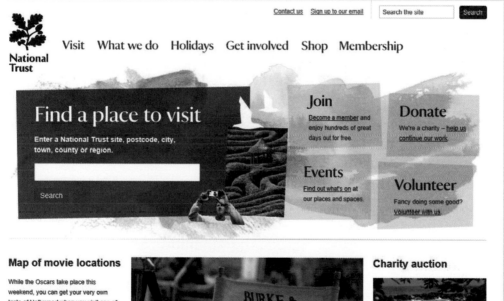

? DID YOU KNOW?
A call to action can be subtle or blatant.

4 Notice that the site also has some less explicit calls to action, including those on the Holidays menu. If you click Camping, you can find out about the National Trust's campsites, but the implicit call to action is clear: make a reservation at one of our campsites.

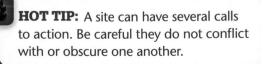

HOT TIP: A site can have several calls to action. Be careful they do not conflict with or obscure one another.

Understand your constraints

You should understand your constraints early in a project. Not understanding your constraints is the largest risk to not completing your website.

1 Consider how much money you have. What is your budget?

2 Consider how much time you have. How long can you take? Even if the project is you creating your homepage, you have constraints. You have a job, hobbies and maybe a few kids. Time spent working on your website is time taken from other activities. You have only so much time in any given day, so you have constraints.

3 Write down your constraints and refer to them often. Use these constraints to remind you that your site must have limits.

4 Use your constraints to plan how you will build your site. For instance, I was under tight time constraints to complete my site (my real site, not the hypothetical one scattered throughout this book), and so I opted to use the Endless CSS template from FreeCSSTemplates.com for my website and the Reference WordPress blog template from FreeWPThemes.net.

5 You must also consider monthly maintenance costs. Updating a site costs time and money. Because I wish to minimise the time required to update my site, I opted for a WordPress blog for posting new content, as WordPress makes updating my blog extremely easy.

🔥 **HOT TIP:** Starting with a content management system (CMS) like WordPress and a pre-made template makes designing, developing and updating your site much easier. Although WordPress is designed for blogs, it is also an excellent tool for building and managing websites.

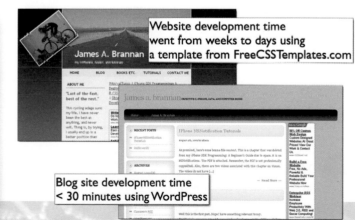

Website development time went from weeks to days using a template from FreeCSSTemplates.com

Blog site development time < 30 minutes using WordPress

🔥 **HOT TIP:** Knowing your constraints helps avoid feature creep. Feature creep is when extra features find their way into your product. It is characterised by 'just one more page' or 'just one more feature'. Over time, these added features cause budget and time overruns and usually cause projects to fail.

Identify a service you can offer users

If you want a really successful site, you need a real service your site can offer its users. Moreover, you need a service that will keep users coming back.

1 Consider how your site can offer a true service.

2 Can your site provide something of value to your target audience like software, documentation or information not easily obtained elsewhere?

3 After determining one or more services, brainstorm: is there a bigger, more valuable service you can offer?

4 Consider adding a user forum where users can share information and create a community out of your site: one example is Bodybuilding.com's user forum.

HOT TIP: Consider providing some way for visitors to interact with the site, perhaps by posting product reviews or comments, or interacting with one another in a discussion forum. This helps form an active community around your site and enables visitors to contribute content that is likely to make your site more attractive to search engines like Google.

DID YOU KNOW?

Do not let this section discourage you. Your site can offer small services that make it much more valuable. For instance, if developing a website for your church, services you might provide include clear directions and a map to your location, a services schedule, contact information and an event calendar. These services, albeit humble, should be what you focus on while designing your site.

HOT TIP: Make sure whatever service you offer is truly valuable to your target audience and is not merely promotional material or an infomercial. Ask yourself, 'Even if the person does not make a purchase, will he or she value the service provided?'

Make sure your ecommerce site offers a service

Successful ecommerce sites usually fill a niche market, selling items hard to obtain at a traditional brick-and-mortar shop. Successful ecommerce sites might sell items much more cheaply than traditional shops or offer a greater selection. To compete on the Web, your ecommerce site must offer a service to users.

1 Consider www.bikeman.com. Although its main goal is to sell products, it offers a valuable service even if a visitor does not buy anything: product reviews, repair instructions and technical information about bicycles and related parts and equipment.

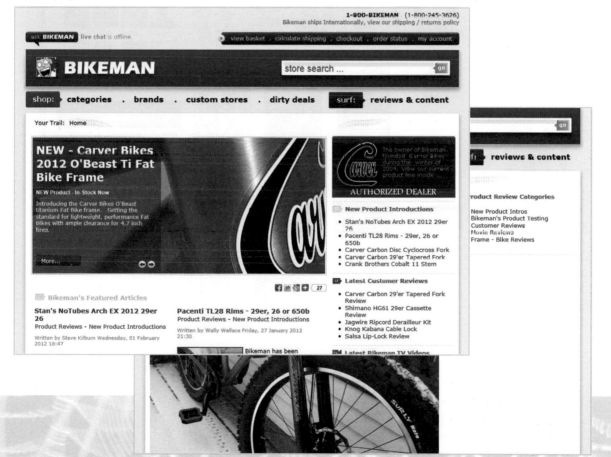

2 Now consider AnimeNation (www.animenation.com). This site offers anime videos and magazines to anime enthusiasts. In addition to offering a huge product line, the site provides news that visitors may find interesting and it hosts anime forums to maintain an active community that draws people who are interested in anime.

When offering a service, make it relevant and valuable

Take care not to offer shallow, self-serving services. Your users will recognise this shallowness immediately.

1 The JamesSpeak hypothetical site illustrates an extremely shallow service. All the site's supposed advice on audio speakers is a sales pitch for the speakers sold through the site.

2 Contrast this with Bodybuilding.com, an ecommerce site that sells nutritional supplements. Notice the extensive articles, forum, exercise database and other features.

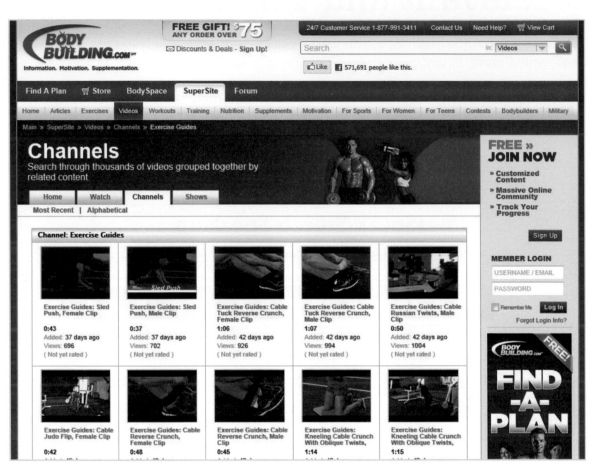

Gather requirements, even if you don't think there are any

Once you know your site's primary mission and the services it is to provide, you should formalise those services into requirements. A requirement is a statement that identifies a necessary feature your site must have. These statements direct how you design and develop your site.

1 Write your requirements in a list. Suppose, after analysing what I wish to accomplish with my personal website, I write the requirements listed in Table 1.2 on page 30. Writing requirements for a small site might seem excessive, but it is not.

2 Compare your requirements list against your goals and the services you wish to offer users.

3 Desires formalised into requirements become website pages. And as you will learn in Chapter 10, these requirements provide tests that you use to ensure your website does what you want it to do.

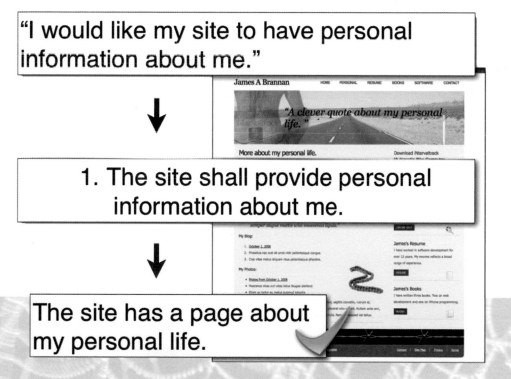

"I would like my site to have personal information about me."

↓

1. The site shall provide personal information about me.

↓

The site has a page about my personal life.

Table 1.2

1	The site shall provide personal information about me.
1.1	The site shall provide a blog.
1.2	The site shall provide photos.
2	The site shall provide a summary of my books.
2.1	The site shall provide a means for users to buy my books.
3	The site shall provide a summary of software I developed.
4	The site shall provide online help for my freeware, iNtervalTrack.
5	The site shall provide my résumé.
6	The site shall provide a means to download iNtervalTrack.
6.1	The site shall require users to register and agree with iNtervalTrack's licence.
7	The site shall use HTML and CSS to present its content.
8	The site shall save user information of users who register for software.

DID YOU KNOW?

Software engineers call this formalisation step *requirements analysis*. Its goal is to gather the functions software must provide if the software is to meet user needs. This step could be formal or informal, depending upon the project's size.

HOT TIP: By writing down requirements, you know exactly what features your site must provide.

Create a use case diagram

A good way to capture user requirements is through a use case diagram. A use case diagram is part of the Unified Modelling Language (UML). Software engineers use UML to design a software system before developing and writing the actual software.

1 Identify your users and add them to this diagram as stick figures.

2 Write the primary activities users perform on your site as use cases.

3 Determine optional activities that extend the primary activities; these activities extend a use case.

4 Determine the sub-activities users must perform to meet a primary activity. These activities are included by the primary activities.

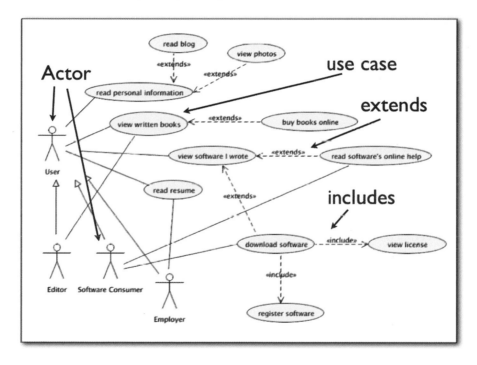

! ALERT: This chapter's use cases are simple. Often use cases involve more extended use cases. For these situations, it helps to list the use cases in numbered steps on paper prior to creating a use case diagram. Refer to any book on UML for more details on use case analysis.

WHAT DOES THIS MEAN?

Google: To conduct an Internet search on a topic or person.

Service: A service is a useful feature, or utility, provided to a site's users. For instance, Flickr offers users a service by allowing them to share photos with one another. Or Wikipedia offers a service to users with its online dictionary.

Blog: A website where an individual regularly posts commentary and other material; the online equivalent to a combined journal and scrapbook.

Content management system (CMS): Software that typically resides online and provides tools for designing, building and maintaining a website or blog and that makes it easy to post and update content.

Ecommerce: Buying and selling goods over the Internet. Ecommerce is a contraction of the words *electronic* and *commerce*.

Cascading Style Sheet (CSS): A design language used by webpages to format content.

CSS template: A pre-designed cascading style sheet that a designer can download and use to control the overall layout, colour scheme and appearance of a site.

Hypertext Markup Language (HTML): A system of tagging the elements, such as headings and paragraphs, that comprise a webpage. Tagging elements helps identify them to browsers, so the browser can determine how to display those elements. In addition, tags enable CSS styles to target specific types of content for formatting.

Web 2.0: Web vernacular for sites that offer user interactive services, where the user is part of a community. For instance, Flickr (www.flickr.com) and YouTube (www.youtube.com) are considered Web 2.0 sites.

? DID YOU KNOW?

Use case diagrams graphically model the results of use case analysis. Use case analysis is similar to requirements analysis, but more specialised. Use cases capture user interaction with the system. The user is called an actor and the user's interaction is called a use case.

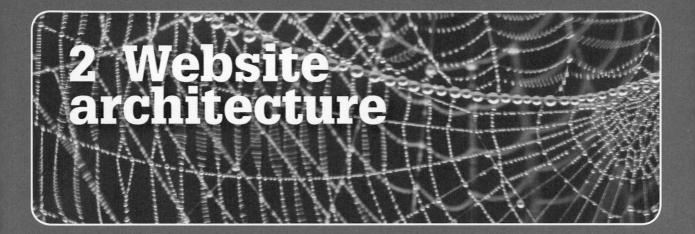

2 Website architecture

Introduction

Once you have a concrete idea about the website you are to build, you create the site's architecture. Start with a blueprint based upon the activities determined in Chapter 1. The blueprints form the site's skeleton or framework. Upon this framework, you later design your site's webpages. This chapter has six primary steps for creating your website architecture. The remaining tasks are best practices to remember while performing these six primary steps shown in the diagram below.

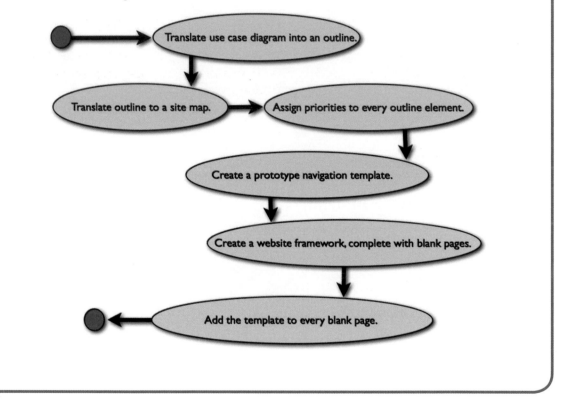

Translate the use case diagram into an outline

The first thing you should do after formalising your use cases is to translate the use case diagram into an outline. Having an outline helps organise the use cases into a logical hierarchy.

1 Create a top-level outline (as shown here) from the use case diagram on page 31.

2 Add email to the outline's top level.

3 Create a second level from the use cases that extend or include the primary use cases.

4 Create a third level for any secondary use cases that require another level. For example, downloading software involves accepting the licence, registering and then physically downloading the software, so you make these three use cases third-level topics.

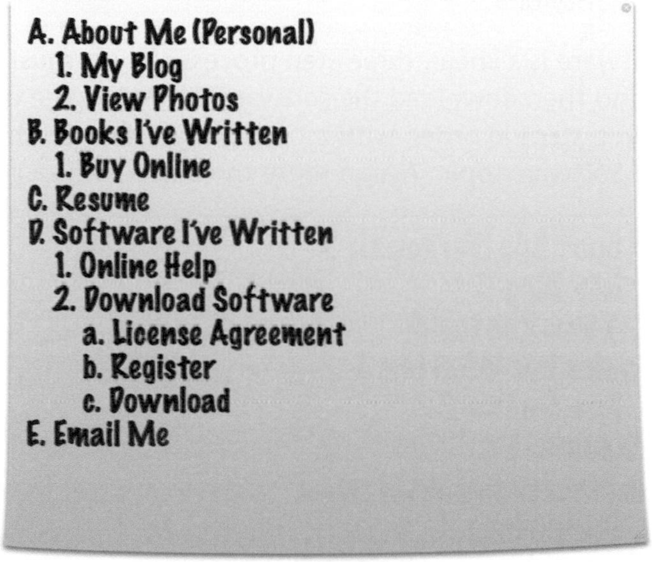

```
A. About Me (Personal)
    1. My Blog
    2. View Photos
B. Books I've Written
    1. Buy Online
C. Resume
D. Software I've Written
    1. Online Help
    2. Download Software
        a. License Agreement
        b. Register
        c. Download
E. Email Me
```

ALERT: Most use cases translate directly to an HTML page, but a few do not. There are no steadfast rules, so use your best judgement.

Assign priorities to every outline element

After translating the use cases into an outline, assign priorities to each outline element. Assigning priorities helps determine an outline's most important topics (pages).

1 Look at the example here. It is important that people can download my software easily. I also want to give employers easy access to my résumé and give editors easy access to my written books. And, of course, I want potential employers and editors with book contracts to contact me, so emailing me is of utmost importance.

2 Assign 'Email Me' a priority of 1. Assign 'Download Software', 'Books I've Written' and 'Résumé' a priority of 1.

3 Discussing my software and my personal information is not so important to me. Assign 'Software I've Written' a priority of 2 and 'About Me' a priority of 3. Because it's not important if users read my blog or view my photos, assign 'My Blog' and 'View Photos' a priority of 3.

4 Downloading software is a linear, three-step process. A user must agree to the licence, register and then download the software. Moreover, he or she must perform these three steps in order, without skipping a step. So these are sub-steps of the Download Software topic. Assign these three sub-steps a priority of 1.

```
A. About Me (Personal) 3
   1. My Blog 3
   2. View Photos 3
B. Books I've Written 1
   1. Buy Online 2
C. Resume  1
D. Software I've Written 2
   1. Online Help 1
   2. Download Software 1
      a. License Agreement 1
      b. Register 1
      c. Download 1
E. Email Me 1
```

Translate the outline to a site map

The outline translates into your site map. A site map is a visual model of a website's pages. The site map should follow the outline's structure.

1 Refer to the sample outline on the previous page. Create a top-level page, My Homepage.

2 Create first-level pages from the top-level topics shown on the previous page. Feel free to change the names.

3 Create second-level pages.

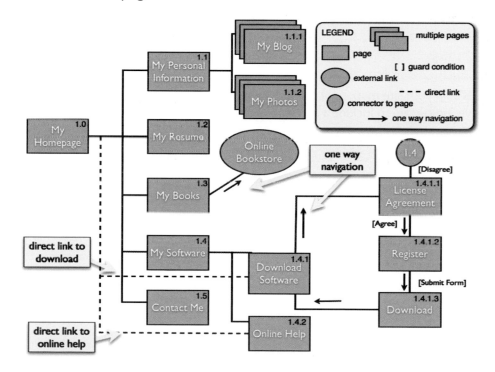

HOT TIP: Number your pages. Referring to a page using a number is easier than referring to a page by its name.

4 Create third-level pages. Note that downloading is a three-step process. First, a user must agree to the licence. Second, a user must register his or her name and email address and then submit this information. Third, the user must click on a direct link to the software's installer. A user must perform this three-step process sequentially, without skipping a step. Indicate this sequential navigation using arrows to show the one-way flow.

5 A user must agree to the licence. Show this required agreement using what is called a guard condition between the 1.4.1.1 and 1.4.1.2 pages. If a user disagrees, the site should return the user to the 1.4 page.

6 Buying one of my books online requires sending a user to an external bookseller such as Amazon, so indicate Online Bookstore as an external link.

7 My blog and photos are topics that will probably grow over time. As they grow, I will probably add new pages. Show the multi-page nature of these pages by using multiple pages in the site map.

ALERT: If your site map is not immediately intuitive, be certain to include a legend explaining all symbols.

HOT TIP: Pages that are important yet two or three levels deep in the outline should have direct links on the top-level home page (see 'Follow the three-click rule', next). For instance, as illustrated on page 36, allowing users to download my software, access online help, and view my résumé is of utmost importance. But only my résumé is a top-level outline element and so the other two elements become direct links, bypassing the site's page hierarchy.

Follow the three-click rule

When designing your site's outline and subsequent site map, remember that users are impatient. If a user cannot find the desired information quickly, he or she will usually look elsewhere. That 'elsewhere' is usually a competitor's site. The three-click rule states that users should never have to click more than three links to reach the desired information.

1 Consider the Food Standards Agency website (www.food.gov.uk), designed primarily for consumers and food industry professionals. When consumers access this site, they are looking for information about food safety.

2 Suppose you are a consumer and want to check if any food allergy alerts have recently been issued. Click the 'Safety and Hygiene' hyperlink. This is the first click.

3 Scan the menu that appears, and find the 'Food allergy' hyperlink and click it (second click). Note that you can also scroll down the Safety and Hygiene page to find the Food allergy hyperlink and hyperlinks to other offerings one level down from it.

4 Skim the page to find the 'Allergy Alerts' hyperlink and click it (third click). The page that appears displays a list of recent allergy alerts along with a link you can click to subscribe and receive food allergy alerts via email.

 SEE ALSO: Not everything can be three clicks. This is where Chapter 1's 'Narrow your purpose to one goal' and 'Have a call to action' best practices are relevant. Be certain that pages most relevant to your site's main goal and pages relevant to what actions you wish users to take are never more than three clicks away.

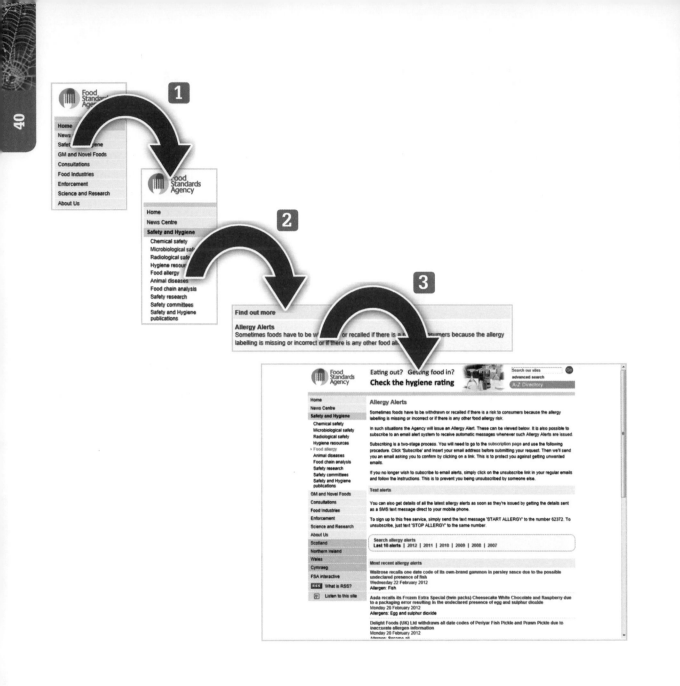

Use sequential navigation when appropriate

Use sequential navigation when you have a series of pages with equivalent importance on the same topic. These pages follow a linear path. Pages in a book's chapter are sequential, as are most magazine articles. You move from page to page, sequentially turning the page from page n to page n+1.

1 This diagram illustrates sequential page navigation.

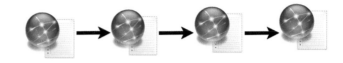

2 Navigate to freecsstemplates. org and navigate through the templates.

3 Note that you are navigating sequentially between pages of templates.

4 Try finding another site that uses sequential navigation. Hint: Google's search results are sequential, as are Flickr's.

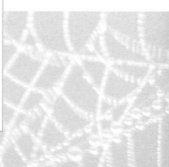

Use external links sparingly and prudently

You usually want visitors to remain on your website as long as possible, especially if you want them to buy something, so use external links (links out to other sites) sparingly. If you want to send users to a different site, be sure to link only to reputable sites and make it clear from the link the destination they should expect.

1 Navigate to the Directgov website (www.direct.gov.uk). Navigate to the job search page and perform a search.

2 Click one of the jobs that appear in the search results.

3 Scroll down and note the external link to Transport Direct. The text accompanying the link provides a clear indication that by clicking the link you will arrive at a site where you can get directions to the job's location.

4 Notice that Directgov contains several links to external sites, but most of these link to sites hosted on subdomains, such as www.businesslink.gov.uk and www.redtapechallenge.cabinetoffice.gov.uk.

? DID YOU KNOW?

Sending a user to a different site implies that the external site meets your approval. Users will judge you and your site by the company you keep, so be sure you associate your site only with those you trust.

Directgov

1

Jobs and Skills search

Search for jobs

Welcome to the Jobcentre Plus job search

Thousands of new jobs available every week. Alternatively, look for voluntary work using the link at the bottom of this page.

Search for jobs by entering a job title, job reference or SOC code, and location.

Job title, job ref or SOC code:

web designer

e.g. receptionist, e.g. all jobs,
e.g. ABC/12345

Postcode or location:

e.g. Sheffield, e.g. S1 2I A

Distance:

15 miles

Search ➡

Job title	Wage	Location	Date posted
▸ FULL TIME WEB DESIGNER Permanent Job No: WOP/41050 SOC Code: 2132	£6 TO £7 PER HOUR	WORKSOP, NOTTINGHAMSHIRE	24/02/2012
▸ WEB DESIGNER Permanent Job No: CVD/103317 SOC Code: 3421	BASED ON SKILLS AND EXPERIENCE	SHEFFIELD, SOUTH YORKHSIRE	14/02/2012
▸ PHP Web Developer Permanent Job No: STH/15977 SOC Code: 2132	£20000 to £25000 Per Annum	Renishaw SHEFFIELD	02/02/2012

Additional information

If you are looking for work, Tax Credits could top up your earnings

This vacancy meets the requirements of the National Minimum Wage Act

If you are unable to apply for the job advertised by the method displayed, due to a health condition or disability, please contact Jobcentre Plus for further assistance.

For more information about tax credits, visit the HM Revenue and Customs website

To find out how to get to this location go to Transport Direct

WHAT DOES THIS MEAN?

Subdomain: A subset of an entire domain that has its own unique website address; for example, if your website has the domain www.yoursite.co.uk, you can set up an ecommerce site at the domain shop.yoursite.co.uk or products.yoursite.co.uk. Subdomains do not cost extra, so you can use them to host multiple sites while paying to register a single domain.

Do not let ads detract from your site's content

One way to use a website to generate revenue is to allow businesses like Google AdSense to display advertising on the site. If you plan on including advertising, keep in mind that ads often drive visitors away, and carefully consider whether the advertising will support or undermine your site's primary goal. If you decide to include advertising, just be sure the ads do not detract too much from your site.

1 Navigate to www.fixedgearfever.com, an online source for bicycle racing on velodromes. Notice it contains a considerable number of advertisements.

2 Note the ads are confined to four locations: the left margin, the right margin, across the page's top (below the page's banner) and across the page's bottom (above the page's housekeeping links). The ads may be distracting, but they do not interfere with access to the site's main content: the discussion forums.

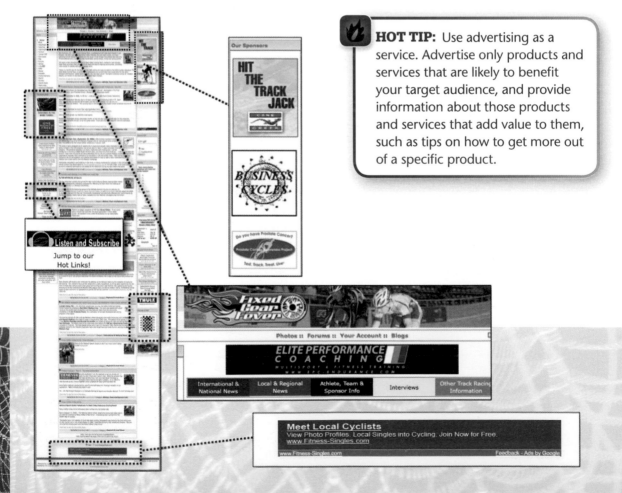

HOT TIP: Use advertising as a service. Advertise only products and services that are likely to benefit your target audience, and provide information about those products and services that add value to them, such as tips on how to get more out of a specific product.

Ensure your site has no dead ends

A dead end is a page that provides no navigation links. The only way a user can navigate back to your site is through the browser's back button. When creating your site's framework, be certain not to create any dead ends.

1 Look at this hypothetical page. As well as being a brilliant design (yes, I am available for freelance design consultation), it illustrates a dead end page.

2 Notice there are only two ways to escape: using your browser's back button or closing your browser window.

HOT TIP: If you use a content management system (CMS) to build your site, it provides options that enable you to easily add navigation elements to your pages, so visitors never reach a dead end.

SEE ALSO: Refer to 'Ensure every page has a page header' and 'Ensure every page has a page footer' in this chapter to avoid this problem entirely.

Do not use under construction pages

Often, developers publish a website before its completion. You really should not publish a site until it is completed, but if you must, then do not use an under construction page as a placeholder for the actual content to be completed. Instead, do not provide the link in the first place.

1 Create an actual draft of each page you want to include on your website.

2 Link to the page only when it is ready to go live.

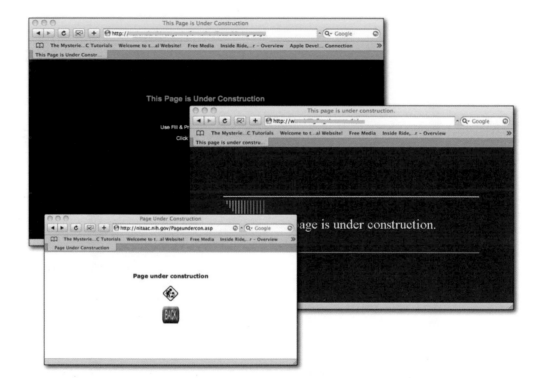

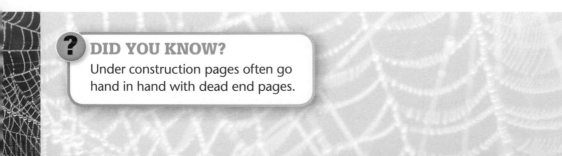

? DID YOU KNOW?

Under construction pages often go hand in hand with dead end pages.

Ensure every page has a page header

A header is the area at the top of a webpage that usually identifies the site. It repeats on most, if not all, webpages across the site. It is the most important element a page has and is vital to creating a consistent site.

1 Navigate to www.pearsoned.co.uk.

2 Note that the logo is in the top left corner. The header contains a navigation bar.

3 Navigate through the site; a similar header repeats across the site.

? DID YOU KNOW?

Experts recommend that within the first four inches of a page's top left corner you place something indicating your identity, such as a logo.

⚠ ALERT: Headers create consistency and usability for users; before modifying the header on different pages, ask if the modification is truly necessary and actually provides navigation context.

Ensure every page has a page footer

Almost as important as the header is the footer, and like the header, the footer should repeat on every page. Footers usually contain 'housekeeping' links to topics such as the site map, terms of site use, copyright and similar topics. The footer also commonly contains information such as last updated, contact information, and sometimes the site's top-level navigation categories.

1 Navigate to the UK government's Department for Culture, Media and Sport homepage (www.culture.gov.uk).

2 Scroll to the page's bottom and notice the footer. Navigate to a couple of the site's internal pages; note the footer is consistent across pages.

Make hyperlinks and icons explicit

You have probably been to at least one website where the navigation was confusing. An easy way to confuse users is by designing navigation links that do not look like hyperlinks.

1 Refer to the two hypothetical pages shown here. Besides being design masterpieces, complete with a scantily clad model, they illustrate ambiguous and explicit icon links.

2 Note that in the first version, although the graphics look like they might be links, until you move your mouse over an icon this is not completely clear.

3 In the second version, the page labels all the graphics with a text hyperlink, allowing you to click the graphic or the text link.

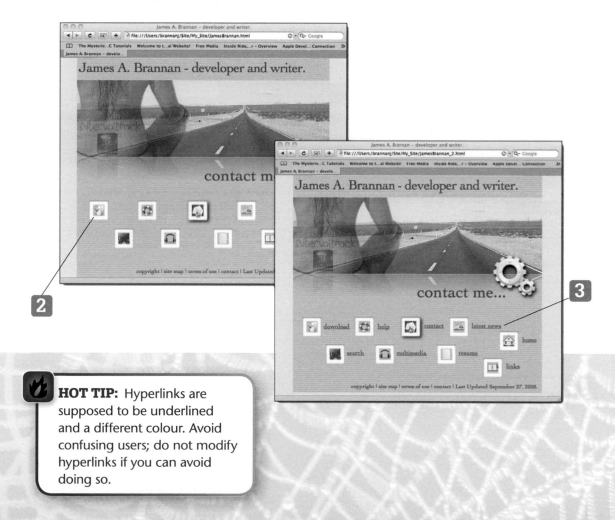

Use breadcrumb trails when designing complex sites

Breadcrumb trails show a user's location within a site. A breadcrumb trail is a single line of text links that traces the path from a website's home to the current page. Each level is a link to the relevant page. The current page is usually not a link in the breadcrumb trail.

1 Refer to page shown here at www.rnib.org.uk. The current page is Laws and standards for websites. This page is four levels deep from the homepage: Home > Professionals > Web Access Centre > Laws and standards.

2 Each hyperlink in the breadcrumb trail is a hyperlink to the level's main page. For instance, clicking 'Web Access Centre' would take you to the Web Access Centre.

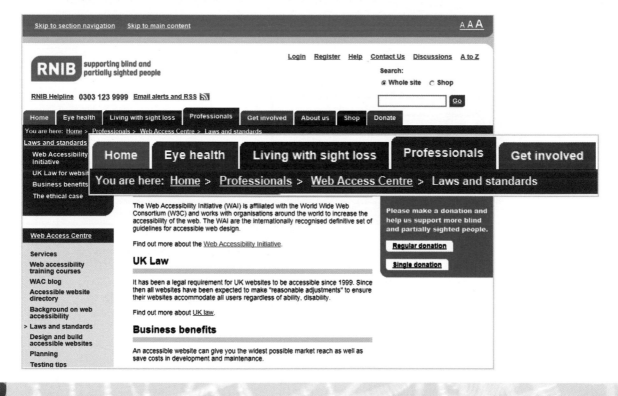

HOT TIP: Breadcrumb trails are an easy way for a lost user to navigate back 'home'.

Always create a site map or site index

If your site is more than a few pages, a site map is one of your site's most important pages. A site map lists your entire site's links on one page. If developing a larger site, consider using an alphabetised site index rather than a site map.

1 Navigate to www.nhsdirect.wales.nhs.uk and click 'Site Map' in the navigation bar.

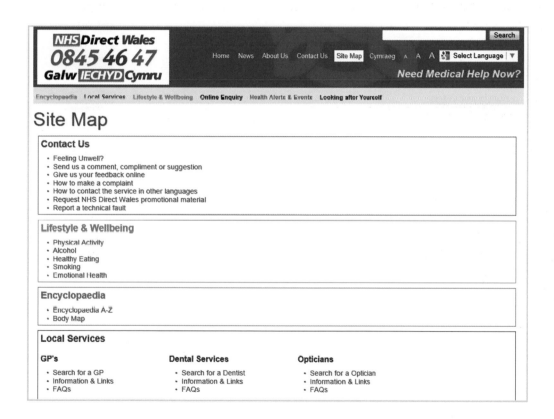

DID YOU KNOW?

Putting all links on a single page helps users navigate more quickly to the desired information. You do not have to include every page on your site, but you should list every major section and subsection.

2 Navigate to www.direct.gov.uk and click 'Site index' in the navigation bar near the top.

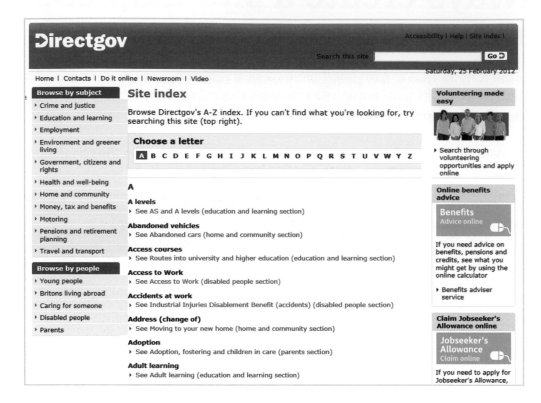

3 Note the similarities and differences between the two. Consider which one's style would be more appropriate for your site.

SEE ALSO: See 'Translate the outline to a site map' on page 37. This site map translates almost directly to the site map you created when first drafting your site, with the subsequent additions and subtractions accounted for.

? DID YOU KNOW?

A site index is exactly like a book's index, only each index term is a hyperlink to the site's relevant page.

Create a prototype navigation template

Creating a prototype navigation template while still developing a site's architecture is often helpful. Clients are impatient and want to see results immediately. And most clients do not consider site map results; they consider webpage results.

1 Navigate to www.freetemplates.org and find the Puzzled CSS template. I base the navigation template shown here on that template.

2 When creating a template, translate the first-level pages into your main navigation menu. Because the names in the map on page 37 are too long, I shortened them when adding them to the template.

HOT TIP: A navigation template can be as simple as a sketch on paper, or a bona-fide template, complete with HTML code and CSS style sheet.

3 Ensure the most important direct links make it onto your template. Downloading my software, accessing online help, reading my résumé and reviewing my books are all important, so I modified the template's right column to include a short description and link for each important action. Every page's right column will repeat these four items.

4 I included 'housekeeping' links at the template's bottom. I added a link to contact me (email), a link to the site map, privacy policy and terms for using my website.

5 Notice what the template lacks. It lacks a secondary navigation menu. A secondary navigation menu is for internal links, as you can see in the AnimeNation's secondary menu shown here.

HOT TIP: Consider starting with a bona-fide template from a site such as freecsstemplates.org.

DID YOU KNOW?

You can place housekeeping links in locations other than a page's bottom. Housekeeping links are often placed near the bottom of the left navigation bar or, in the case of a 'Contact Us' link, in the upper right corner of a page.

Create a website framework, complete with blank pages

Creating a website is challenging, akin to decorating your house. You arrange and rearrange until everything looks just right. Now, imagine you had to worry about building your house at the same time as you decorated it. Well, rather than building your website at the same time as you decorate it, why not build it first?

1 Create a framework of all the top-level pages in your site. Create a folder hierarchy to hold the site's pages and images.

2 Add dummy pages for every topic in your outline.

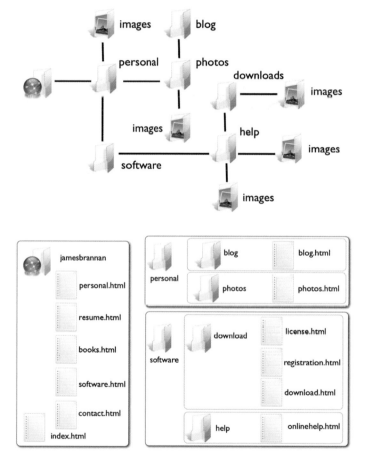

ALERT: UNIX, Linux and Mac OSX are case sensitive. While a resource named myresource. gif and MyResource.gif on Windows are the same file, on UNIX, Linux and OSX these are two distinct files. Most commercial web service providers use Linux or UNIX machines, so if developing on Windows, be careful with your filename and directory name case.

3 Add the template to every page, and fix the hyperlinks between every page. You then have a functioning site, albeit devoid of content. Now you can focus on decorating rather than building and decorating simultaneously.

? DID YOU KNOW?

Adding blank pages might seem wasteful to you, but for me this is a crucial step. This step helps me envision the pages I am to build. It is an easy step: for every topic create a blank HTML page.

⚠ ALERT: You should not be worried about page-specific content, only template items such as titles and hyperlinks. Remember, you can add page-specific elements later; for now just get the navigation template working. By this stage, you should have an entire site where each page reflects its content and its hyperlinks are fully functioning.

3 Writing your text

Introduction

On the Web, content is king. Relevant information that addresses the needs of the targeted audience attracts visitors from around the world and keeps them coming back. Quality content also helps establish the site as a reliable and trusted resource for information on a specific topic, so you must strive to deliver quality content that is well written and error free. Vapid, error-riddled copy, regardless of how beautifully designed the website is, drives away users and ruins the site's reputation.

Consider blogging

Even if you are designing a static website, you should consider blogging: writing and publishing fresh content on a regular basis and inviting visitors to comment on it. Although blogging started as a personal-publishing tool, it has developed into a valuable business tool that enables individuals and businesses to establish credibility and trust, build a following and become more attractive to search engines like Google. Publishing content to a blog is very easy.

1 Install a blogging platform, such as WordPress.

2 After logging on, click 'Posts' and click 'Add New Post'.

3 Type and format the content as you would in a word processing application, and click 'Publish'.

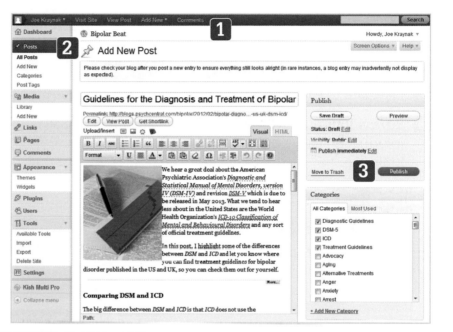

ALERT: Blogging can become a big responsibility and a huge time commitment. Users generally expect fresh content to be posted at least twice a week, and they often expect and sometimes demand responses to their comments. If you do not have the time, energy and enthusiasm to make and keep a long-term commitment, you are probably better off not blogging.

HOT TIP: Most website hosting services have tools for installing a blogging platform that can get your blog up and running in a matter of minutes.

WHAT DOES THIS MEAN?

Blog: An abbreviation of web log, a blog is a website that contains regular (usually weekly to daily) posts and typically enables visitors to respond to posts with their own comments.

Ensure your site contains quality content

Although you and your clients want a website that is attractive, engaging and easy to navigate, the most important component of any site is its content. Content may include introductory text, product descriptions, testimonials, reviews, news, instructions, discussions, games and so on, and it can come in a variety of media, including text, images, audio, video and software. What you choose to offer on a site depends on your target audience's needs and desires and the goals you hope to accomplish through the site.

1 Pick five sites, any sites, which you visit regularly.

2 Navigate to each in turn. Ask yourself what it is about the site that draws you to it.

3 Review four sites I visit frequently, shown here. I visit all four for the service or information each provides. I visit these sites for textual information, not their design brilliance.

Chunk your information into bite-size pieces

Chunking information is a term that describes breaking information into small, easily processed information chunks. Psychologists discovered that people tend to learn best by learning in discrete units, or chunks. Moreover, they discovered that the maximum number of chunks that the human brain can keep in storage at any one time is about seven.

1 Break information into small, easy to read and process chunks.

2 Label each chunk with descriptive text. This enables readers to quickly find what they want and skip the rest.

3 Arrange chunks into logical groups, such as most similar or most recent.

4 Limit the amount of information in each chunk, while providing users with the option of viewing more.

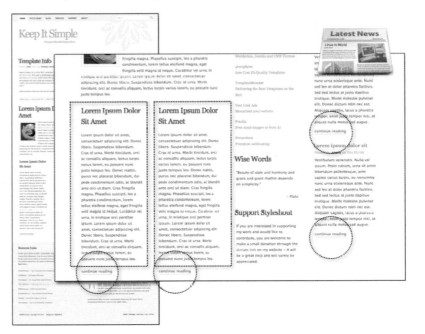

🔥 **HOT TIP:** Avoid paragraphs, especially long ones, where possible. Instead, present items in lists. If each list item is longer than one sentence, label each item with a few descriptive words in bold at the beginning, so readers can quickly skim the list to find what they want.

❓ **DID YOU KNOW?**
This page is a CSS template entitled 'Keep It Simple' and is available at www.styleshout.com.

Write like a journalist

Journalists write using an inverted pyramid structure. The first few sentences are the most important. In these few sentences, you must tell the reader: who, what, when, where, why and how. After conveying these six pieces of information, you can then tell the story in more depth. This writing style fits perfectly with web writing style.

1 Consider the template from the last section. The content is chunked. Each item on the page consists of one or two paragraphs, followed by a 'continue reading' link to more detailed content on other pages. Each chunk is sized to tell the reader quickly who, what, when, where, why and how. If the user wishes more detail, he or she can click the link.

2 Notice the Featured column along the template's right side, shown here. The top paragraph is only 61 words before linking to the 'continue reading' link.

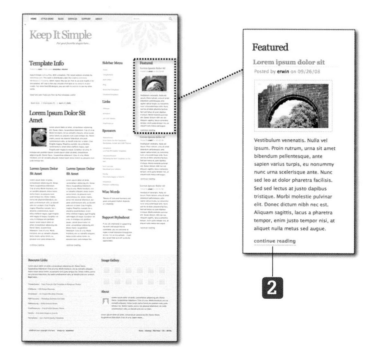

2

3 Now navigate to the NHS website at www.nhsdirect.nhs.uk, click 'Check your symptoms' in the navigation bar near the top and click 'General health'. Notice how the site uses lists, headings and small amounts of text, along with links that users can click to access additional content.

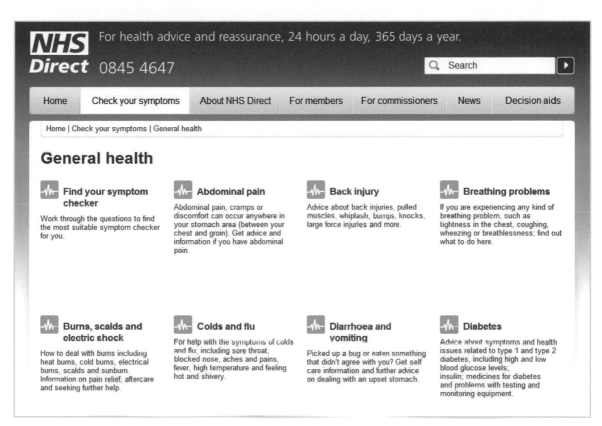

HOT TIP: When using a template such as Keep It Simple, rather than changing the paragraphs' lengths on the homepage, consider modifying your content to match the length. This ensures your content stays concise. Use the 'continue reading' links to provide more information on interior webpages.

HOT TIP: Detail is good, but present the who, what, when, where, why and how in about 50 words or less on your homepage and provide the remaining detail on another page. By the way, make those 50 words count; hook the reader so he or she is compelled to click the link for more detail.

Write descriptive headings and subheadings

So, you followed the previous section's advice and wrote all your information in 50-word chunks with a hyperlink to the more detailed information. Many visitors will not even read those 50 words. You must write descriptive and compelling headings and subheadings for the users who skim.

1 Notice this hypothetical webpage (using the free TechJunkie CSS template by www.styleshout.com). The page summarises the story and provides a link for users who wish to continue reading. It also provides a subheading to pique a user's interest in the story. A user can easily skim the page and get a general understanding of its content.

2 Now notice the contents page opposite. It uses headings, subheadings and several callouts. Together the headings, subheadings and callouts provide a complete article summary. A skimmer can easily get the gist of the story without reading every word.

ALERT: Non-reading users are not stupid, nor are they shallow. They are busy. These users choose not to read, and no matter how enticing you make those 50 words, many will not read them.

HOT TIP: Callouts, a common technique in printed media, work well in web content.

Persuade users with subtle techniques

Convincing users to perform a site's call to action requires subtle and not so subtle persuasion techniques, including framing, problem-solving, comparison and contrast, expert opinion and emotional manipulation.

1 Frame issues in a way that is likely to make your audience more receptive. One way to reframe an issue is to shift focus from the current situation which may be controversial to a positive vision of a future point in time.

2 Refer to the hypothetical site shown here. Car salespeople often frame their sales pitch differently for different audiences. For families, the salesperson may focus on interior space and safety features. For environment or budget conscious drivers, the salesperson may focus on fuel efficiency and emissions.

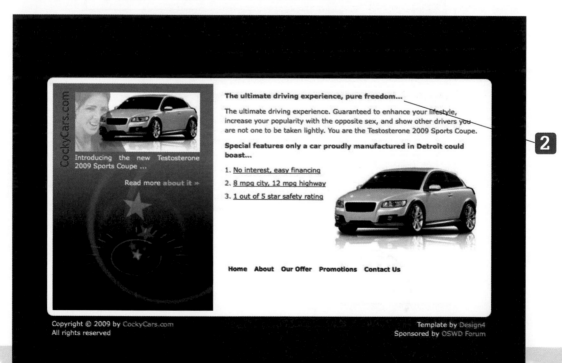

3 Consider persuading your site's users by providing a problem and a solution. Many users search the Web to find answers to questions and solutions to problems. Clearly state the problem up front and then follow up with the solution. Of course, the solution should agree with your call to action, such as order our product, sign up for our newsletter, volunteer for our cause or donate.

4 Choose an appropriate formality level for your message and your audience. You must understand how formal you should or should not be. If trying to persuade someone to invest financially, for example, you want a formal site that exudes confidence and professionalism.

5 Consider persuading your users by empathising with them. Political candidates are masters of this technique.

> **ALERT:** These persuasion techniques are effective for whatever you happen to be promoting and for any call to action. Whether you are building a church website to attract new members to the congregation or a site to sell nutritional supplements, you need to persuade your target audience that whatever you are promoting benefits them in some way. By practising these techniques effectively, you improve your website's ability to attain its goals.

? DID YOU KNOW?

The hypothetical webpage shown opposite is based upon the Car CSS template by Design4, and is downloaded from Open Source Web Design (www.oswd.org).

Prefer simple to complex and edit your writing

When writing copy for your site, keep it simple and direct and edit carefully to eliminate errors and awkward wording. Forced sophistication is transparent and muddies writing. Instead, opt for simple, precise words, sentences and paragraphs over complex. Once you have written the words, edit them. Poor grammar and spelling detract from your site's purpose and undermine its authority. Ensure your spelling and grammar are correct.

1 Look at the My Musings webpage. Notice the forced sophistication; is it convincing?

2 Now look at the My Dilema page. The spelling and grammatical errors detract greatly from the site's content.

? DID YOU KNOW?

My personal recommendation is a book entitled *Edit Yourself* by Bruce Ross-Larson. His company website, www.clearwriter.com, provides online training and links to all his books for sale on amazon.co.uk.

Ensure meaning is intuitive on important items

Labels, buttons, headers, hyperlinks and other important items should be labelled intuitively. The text on a hyperlink should illustrate rather than conceal the link's purpose. Follow any conventions in place for labelling buttons. For example, standard practice for most forms is to include a Submit and Cancel button, so use those labels unless you have a very good reason for using something else.

1 Revisit the hypothetical webpage on page 68. Pretentious labels replace what should be clearly marked hyperlinks.

2 Now consider the labels' meanings as on the page shown here. Pretentious labels should be changed to clear hyperlinks.

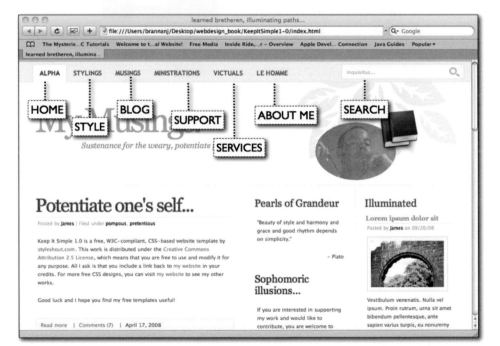

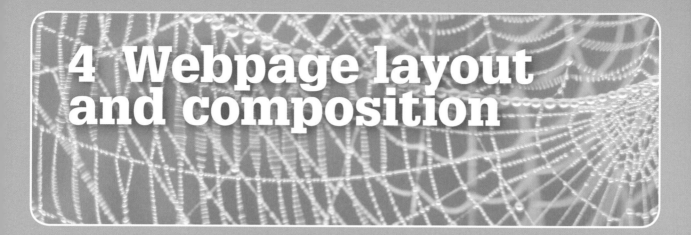

4 Webpage layout and composition

Introduction

Now that you have your site's architecture mapped out and have plenty of relevant, engaging content to offer, you are ready to begin designing the layout and presentation of individual pages. Successful websites do not require design on par with a graphics art magazine. You can design a much more modest site that is quite pleasing and successful. The key is to make a page's design complement its content, helping users navigate through your site and access what it offers more easily.

Place important information above the fold line

In web design, the *fold line* is the onscreen line beyond which the user must scroll down to view additional content. When designing webpages, you generally want the most important content displayed above the fold line, where users are likely to encounter it first. (Keep in mind that screen resolution determines the position of the fold line, so it may be higher or lower for different users.)

1 Navigate to www.wwf.org.uk. Notice that important information is placed above the fold regardless of whether the page is viewed in 1024x768 or 800x600 resolution.

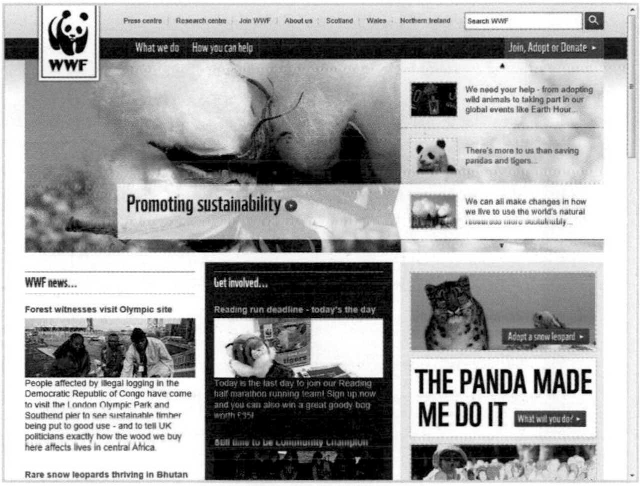

1024x768

800x600

HOT TIP: One way you can entice people to scroll below the fold is by placing interesting content that overlaps the fold line.

SEE ALSO: See page 81 for more details on screen resolution.

2 Notice the hypothetical site for a motorcycle club. To ensure people scroll below the fold line, I place a woman with an exposed shoulder just above the fold line, leaving her remainder below the fold line. Nine out of 10 men and more than a few women will now scroll to the page's base.

Make pages printable

Some users who visit your site are likely to read the text onscreen and be done with it. Others, however, will want to print a copy for future reference or because they prefer reading it on paper. Accommodating all readers' needs is essential in giving your site a global appeal, so provide two versions of every page, one for reading onscreen and one for printing.

1 Create a separate print.css style sheet to format the text for printing.

2 Create styles for any elements you do not want printed that include the declaration 'display: none;'

3 Reference the location of the print.css file in your webpage HTML between the <head></head> tags near the top.

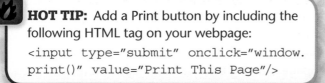

HOT TIP: Add a Print button by including the following HTML tag on your webpage:

```
<input type="submit" onclick="window.
print()" value="Print This Page"/>
```

Use grid theory

Almost all print layouts use a grid to lay out the page. The same is true for well designed webpages. A grid is exactly what it sounds like: it is an invisible framework consisting of intersecting rows and columns that you use to position your page's elements.

1 Draw a grid onscreen or on paper to create a matrix of squares.

2 Draw the various webpage elements you plan to include on each page, assigning each element the desired number of squares.

Logo	Header	
	Navigation Bar	
Secondary Menu		Image
	Main Content Area	
		Preview
	Footer	

HOT TIP: Consider using wireframe software, such as Mockingbird (gomockingbird.com), to design the framework for your pages.

WHAT DOES THIS MEAN?

Grid: An invisible matrix composed of squares.

Wireframe: Skeletal framework for a webpage showing the location of each element.

Violate a page's grid to draw attention to an element

An easy way to draw a user's attention to a certain screen area is by violating the page's natural grid. When used sparingly, violating a page's symmetry can enhance the design of your page.

1 Consider violating the grid's symmetry to draw attention to an element and produce stunning designs, as in the Sweet Garden template from www.freetemplates.org, shown here.

2 Maintain balance in asymmetrical designs by counterweighing larger, heavier elements with smaller, lighter items that take up more space or are placed at a greater distance from the centreline.

ALERT: Asymmetrical designs still require balance. For example, if the right two-thirds of a page are packed with text, you may need a heavy, dense graphic in the left third to counterbalance it.

ALERT: Be careful when violating the grid – practise subtlety.

Emphasise what is important

When designing a webpage, you often have some elements that are more important than others, such as an advertisement that promotes a sale or a link to click to sign up for a free newsletter. Decide which are the most important elements on a page and then emphasise them.

1 Consider placing important elements where visitors are most likely to look: near the top left side of the page. Refer to the Anime Nation webpage shown here. What is the first thing you notice? I bet it is the 'DVD/Blu-ray collection sale'.

2 Use bright, bold colours that are likely to attract attention.

HOT TIP: After the header and left menu, you should place the page's most important content in the top left corner. Moreover, you might consider emphasising it in some way.

DID YOU KNOW?

Placing the 'Special Price Today Only!' or 'Buy Now!' prominently in the top left corner (just below the header and to the left of any side navigation) is a common ecommerce design technique.

Prominently display your purpose, or have a tagline

Design your site in a way that makes its purpose clear by including a mission statement or tagline, or conveying the message by way of the content on each page. Ecommerce sites seldom contain a mission statement, but the purpose of such sites is clear: to help shoppers find products they want and need.

1 Navigate to the Campaign against Euro-federalism website at www.caef.org.uk. Notice the site states the organisation's purpose directly below the banner.

2 Navigate to the Directgov website (www.direct.gov.uk) and notice it states the site's purpose immediately below the logo in the upper left corner of the page.

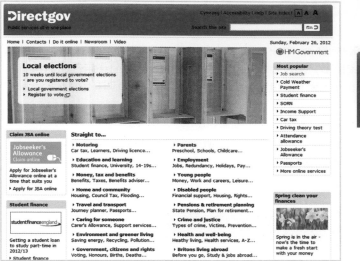

3 Navigate to the UK Department of Health's website (www.dh.gov.uk). The homepage displays the department's purpose. Now click each main link and notice that each page displays its own purpose.

Design for a maximum screen resolution of 1024x768

Always design for a maximum screen resolution of 1024x768. Conservatively, you might consider 800x600, depending upon your target users. But realistically, these days most people's computers display at 1024x768.

1 Notice the webpage shown here. This site is designed for a 1900x1200 screen resolution. On a monitor with a maximum 1024x768 screen resolution, a user must scroll vertically to view the entire page's content.

1900x1200 resolution

1024x768 resolution

Photos for grandma to view on her old 640x480 Monitor

HOT TIP: Always test pages using a 1024x768 screen resolution. If conservative, use 800x600 to test.

SEE ALSO: Some users might have lower resolutions. Some web design experts still recommend 800x600. To avoid this problem entirely, refer to the 'Use a centred layout' section in this chapter and see the centred, liquid layout.

2 Contrast the second example with the first. The Quartz Storage page is designed for a 1024x768 screen resolution. On monitors that can display higher resolutions, the page still looks good.

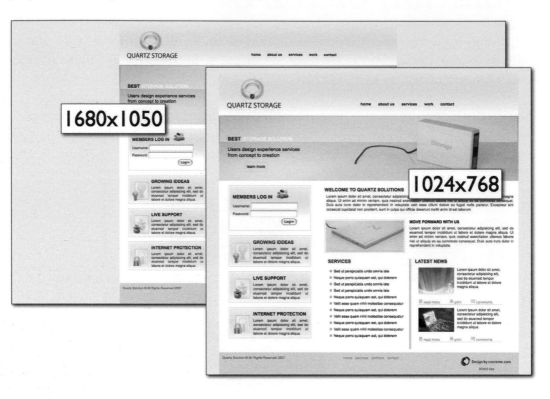

? DID YOU KNOW?

Different computers might display using lower resolutions. During the early to mid 1990s, the standard was designing for a 640x480 screen resolution. As graphic technology improved, the target resolution became 800x600. Today, the standard is 1024x768 and climbing towards something more along the lines of 1600x900.

Know the difference between fixed, liquid and elastic layouts

Cascading style sheets (CSS) apply formatting to webpages to control the overall layout, font styles and size, colours and more. With CSS, you can create different types of page layout, including fixed, liquid and elastic.

1. To create a fixed layout, specify the dimensions of all elements in pixels or another specific unit. As the browser's viewport shrinks, the page remains unchanged.

2. To create a liquid layout, specify column widths as percentages. As the browser's viewport shrinks, columns narrow and the content wraps to accommodate the narrower columns.

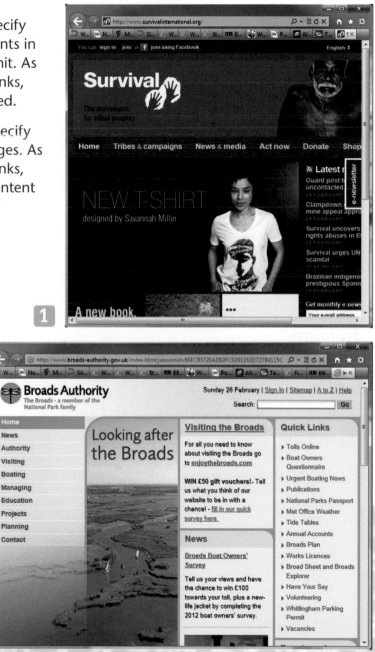

3 To create an elastic layout, specify column and box dimensions in *em* units and use percentages to size text and other contents, so as the viewpoint changes size, everything on the page is resized accordingly.

3

ALERT: If developing a site for a public agency, use a liquid or elastic layout to accommodate users with outdated browsers.

HOT TIP: CSS3 has proposed a flexible box model that enables you to specify whether a box is flexible and the relative sizes of boxes on a page, so the browser can resize boxes for different displays and window dimensions. Here is an example:

```
#sidebar1 {box-flex:0; width:180px; }

#sidebar2 {box-flex:1; min-width:180px; }

#content {box-flex:2; }
```

This tells the browser to make sidebar1 180 pixels wide and not flexible, make sidebar2 a minimum of 180 pixels larger if size permits and make the content column twice as wide as sidebar2.

Use a centred layout

A centred layout helps provide a consistent, balanced view for all users regardless of the display size. So, for example, if you design a fixed width page that is 800 pixels wide, the page is centred in the browser window whether it is displayed at 1600x900, 1024x768 or 800x600. If it were not centred, content would appear far left when viewed in a window at 1600x900 or 1024x768, leaving a lot of white space on the right.

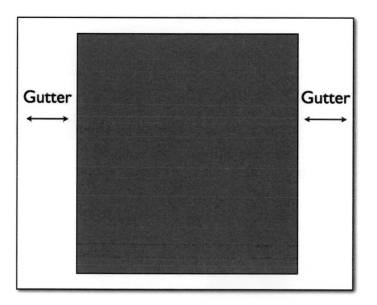

1 Refer to the hypothetical page shown in four versions on the next page. It uses a centred fixed layout. All four figures show the web browser maximised. The top page is at 1680x1050 resolution, the second is at 1024x768 resolution, the third at 800x600 and the last at 640x480. Notice the content section's width remains unchanged, although the 640x480 screen resolution does require scrolling.

2 As an aside, notice that the top page shows the background image's seam. Remember, users might have higher screen resolutions than yours, so be certain your page looks good at higher screen resolutions.

1680x1050

1024x768

800x600

640x480

3 Compare the fixed layout pages with the same pages using a centred liquid layout (see overleaf). As the screen resolution becomes smaller, the content wraps to accommodate the loss in space.

4 Finally, look at the webpage below. Notice the header repeats horizontally because the page is wider than the header image. A common strategy is using a liquid layout, with a fixed maximum width. For instance, in all the preceding webpages, the pages use a maximum width of 720 pixels, the same width as the header graphic. By stating a maximum width, I ensure the header graphic does not repeat in wider browser viewports. This webpage does not specify a maximum width and so the text widens to take most of the browser's viewport and the header's background image repeats.

? DID YOU KNOW?

Centred layout can be liquid or fixed. If fixed, you typically choose the content to be slightly narrower than 1024 pixels or 800 pixels, depending upon if you are targeting 1024x768 or 800x600 displays. If liquid, you specify a percentage less than 100%, allowing the centred content to expand or contract as your browser's viewport resizes.

? DID YOU KNOW?

The hypothetical webpage is based upon the CSS template, Coffee-N-Creme by Arcsin, downloaded from Open Source Web Design (www.oswd.org). The photos are from Flickr. The background and cave are images by James Emery, the faded Anasazi cliff dwelling is a modified photo by Caitlyn Williams and the pottery photo is by Mark Helms. All are released under the Creative Commons Attribution licence.

1680x1050

1024x768

800x600

640x480

5 Using web colour effectively

Introduction

When developing a website, you usually create a colour palette containing four or five colours. You then limit the colour combinations on your pages to the colours in the palette. By consistently applying colours, your website's pages are visually appealing and consistent. Consistent colour usage makes sites easier to navigate and contributes significantly to the site's brand identity.

Important: Most web design books begin by reviewing the colour wheel, primary colours, secondary colours and tertiary colours. This book explains colour theory basics. If you want to learn more about colour theory, and how to create colour palettes from scratch, there are ample online resources. In this book I focus more on using an available tool to make colour selections for you. I have enough trouble coordinating my wardrobe; these tools can do a much better job coordinating my webpage colours.

Have a basic understanding of colour values

Colour values are names or numbers that indicate to a computer which colour to display onscreen. For basic colours, you can use the colour's name. For more subtle hues and shades, you use values that tell the computer which basic colours and hues to mix, and with certain values how rich or light to make the colours.

1 Notice this basic colour chart, which lists colour values according to name, hex value, RGB value and HSL value.

2 Search the Web for 'web colour chart'.

3 Note that the Web has numerous colour charts to help you choose the right colour.

Colour	Colour name	Hex Value	RGB Value	HSL Value
	black	#000000	0,0,0	0°,0%,0%
	blue	#0000FF	0,0,255	240°,100%,100%
	grey	#808080	128,128,128	0°,0%,50%
	green	#008000	0,128,0	120°,100%,25%
	lightblue	#ADD8E6	173,216,230	195°,53%,79%
	lightgrey	#D3D3D3	211,211,211	0°,0%,83%
	lime	#00FF00	0,255,0	120°,100%,50%
	magenta	#FF00FF	255,0,255	300°,100%,50%
	maroon	#800000	128,0,0	0°,100%,25%
	orange	#FFA500	255,165,0	39°,100%,50%
	pink	#FFC0CB	255,192,203	350°,100%,88%
	purple	#800080	128,0,128	300°,100%,25%
	red	#FF0000	255,0,0	0°,100%,50%
	violet	#EE82EE	238,130,238	300°,76%,72%
	whitesmoke	#F5F5F5	245,245,245	0°,0%,96%
	yellow	#FFFF00	255,255,0	60°,100%,50%

Red	Green	Blue	HEX	Color Name	Lum	Hue	Sat	Lig	Color
93	138	168	#5D8AA8	Air Force Blue	52	204	30	51	
240	248	255	#F0F8FF	Alice Blue	97	208	100	97	
227	38	54	#E32636	Alizarin	50	355	77	52	
229	43	80	#E52B50	Amaranth	53	348	78	53	
255	191	0	#FFBF00	Amber	78	45	100	50	
164	198	57	#A4C639	Android Green	70	73	55	50	
141	182	0	#8DB600	Apple Green	62	74	100	36	
251	206	177	#FBCEB1	Apricot	85	24	90	84	
127	255	212	#7FFFD4	Aquamarine	88	160	100	75	
75	83	32	#4B5320	Army Green	30	69	44	23	
59	68	75	#3B444B	Arsenic	26	206	12	26	
233	214	107	#E9D66B	Arylide Yellow	82	51	74	67	
178	190	181	#B2BEB5	Ash Grey	73	135	8	72	
135	169	107	#87A96B	Asparagus	60	93	26	54	
255	153	102	#FF9966	Atomic Tangerine	71	20	100	70	
109	53	26	#6D351A	Auburn	27	20	61	26	
0	127	255	#007FFF	Azure	57	210	100	50	
137	207	240	#89CFF0	Baby Blue	78	199	77	74	
161	202	241	#A1CAF1	Baby Blue Eyes	79	209	74	79	
244	194	194	#F4C2C2	Baby Pink	83	0	69	86	
255	209	42	#FFD12A	Banana Yellow	83	47	100	58	

DID YOU KNOW?

CSS3 supports four different ways to specify colour values:

- **Name:** You can reference common colours by name, such as red, green, blue and purple.
- **RGB value:** An RGB value describes a mixture of different hues of red, green and blue. Each colour has 256 hues, numbered 0 to 255. You create a colour by specifying the three colour values – for example, 176,48,96 for maroon.
- **Hex code:** A hexadecimal (hex) code consists of six characters that represent a colour. Each code is a combination of numbers (0–9) and/or letters (A–F) – for example, #B03060 for maroon. Each two-digit combination is equivalent to a 0–255 RGB value, so B0 in hex is 176 in RGB.
- **HSL value:** An HSL value specifies the hue (colour) as a degree on the colour wheel (0–360) and saturation (intensity) and value (lightness) as percentages (0–100%).

HOT TIP: CSS3 supports a fourth alpha colour value for opacity (0.0 to 1.0) to make colours more or less transparent for layering objects. An HSLA colour value may look like 240,35%,50%,0.4 to produce 40% opaque blue. The RGBA equivalent would be 83,83,172,0.4.

HOT TIP: Google 'RGB colour converter' to find sites that convert colour values from one type to another – for example, RGB to hex or HSL.

Understand colour theory essentials

To ensure the colours you choose look good together, you should understand the essentials of colour theory and the colour wheel.

1 Use a colour wheel, like the one shown here, to determine if colour combinations will be appealing.

2 Choose complementary colours (directly across from one another) for an appealing design with high contrast.

3 Choose a split complementary colour scheme (one colour along with the two colours next to the colour directly across from it) for a high-contrast design with more variation.

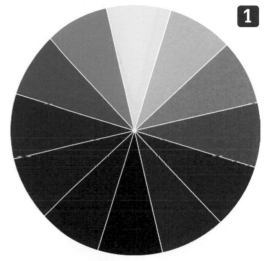

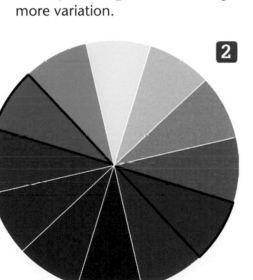

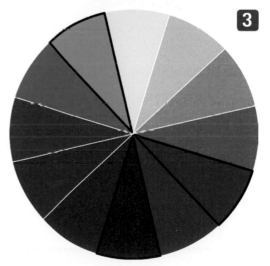

4 Choose analogous colours (next to one another) for an appealing design with less contrast.

5 Choose a triadic colour scheme (three colours equidistant from each other) for a balanced rich design with less contrast.

4
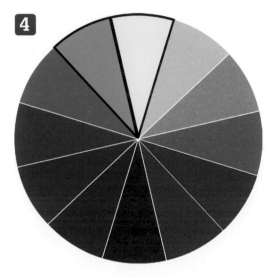

5
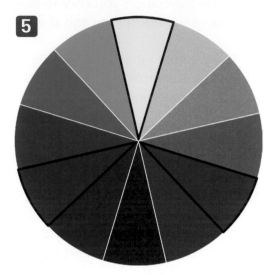

HOT TIP: Achromatic (grayscale) and monochromatic (one colour plus black and white) can be a great choice depending on the site's purpose and tone.

ALERT: Different cultures place different meaning on colours. For instance, in the east white is associated with mourning, whereas in the west white is associated with purity, peace and everything that is good.

? DID YOU KNOW?

Colours are often described as 'cool' and 'warm'. Cool colours range from green to blue to some darker shades of purple. Warm colours range from violet to red (hot) to orange, yellow and even lighter shades of green. You see plenty of holiday, spa, cruise ship and financial websites with cool, relaxing colour schemes. Restaurants, discotheques, casinos and kids' websites often use warm colour schemes.

Use a tool to generate a colour palette

Instead of guessing whether colours are complementary or analogous, consider using a colour palette generator, such as Adobe Kuler.

1 Navigate to kuler.adobe.com and click 'Create'.

2 Choose a colour rule, such as Analogous or Complementary.

3 Drag the big circle on the colour wheel to specify the desired base colour. (You can drag the circle closer to the centre of the colour wheel to mute the colour.)

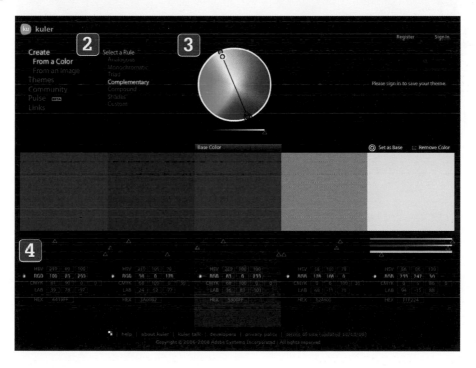

4 Record the colour values for your palette.

HOT TIP: The Web has several free colour palette generators, including Color Scheme Designer (colorschemedesigner.com), Color Schemer Online (www.colorschemer. com/online.html) and ElvanOnline (colorschemegenerator.com).

HOT TIP: If you see a colour you like on a website, you can use a free tool like ColorZilla (www.colorzilla. com) for the Firefox web browser to find the colour's colour value.

Generate a colour palette from a photograph

If your site design includes an image in the header, consider generating your colour palette using the colours in that image. Adobe Kuler makes the job very easy.

1 Navigate to kuler.adobe.com and create an account to log in.

2 From the left menu select 'Create', 'From an Image', and upload an image. I uploaded a photo I took in Denmark.

3 Notice the choices under Select a Mood. You have several choices, depending upon the mood you wish to create. Creating a page about Samba? Choose Colorful or Bright. An information site? Choose Muted. A site about gang violence and poverty's horrors? Choose Deep or Dark.

4 Drag the circles on the image to choose specific colours, if desired.

5 Type a name for your palette in the 'Title' box, click 'Public' or 'Private', and click 'Save'.

6 Click the button with the sliders on it (next to the trash can button).

7 Record the colour values for your palette.

Denmark by timco378

6

Created: 2012.02.27 at 10:45 AM
Last Edited: 2012.02.27 at 10:45 AM
Rated: 0 (0 votes)
Favorited by: 0 members
Downloaded: 0 times
Public: No
Theme Link: http://kuler.adobe.com/#themeID/1788585
Tags:
Make this my avatar

Less Info ▼

Report a Concern

Comments: 0   💬 **Add Comment**

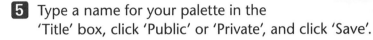

HOT TIP: Mouse over a colour swatch for additional options related to that colour, including the option to remove the colour from the scheme or set it as the base colour. You can also drag the sliders below each colour to fine-tune it.

Use your colour palette consistently across pages

This advice should be common sense, but surprisingly it is often ignored. Do not change your colour palette midway through your website. Every page should use the same colour palette.

1 Look at the webpages here. These two masterpieces are originals, not based upon a downloaded CSS template. I also did not use a tool like Adobe Kuler, instead relying upon my artistic sensibilities.

2 Notice the colour difference between page one and page two. The difference is as jarring as my favourite striped shirt and plaid tie I wear together when applying for web designer jobs.

HOT TIP: Always use an external CSS template to apply text colours and background colours consistently to every page on your site.

Choose colours to match your site's mood

This is another topic that should be common sense, yet it is important enough to state as a separate best practice. Your colour choice should reflect the mood you wish to convey. A tool like Kuler Desktop makes selecting a colour palette to reflect a certain mood much easier.

1 Suppose you wanted to create a sombre, dark site devoted to horror films. What colours should you choose?

2 Start Adobe Kuler and enter 'death' into the search bar, and then review the colours. The swatch, entitled appropriately enough 'death', looks promising.

3 Enter 'horror' into the search bar and review the colours returned. The swatch entitled 'gothic' seems a good choice.

4 Now search for 'circus', and Kuler returns bright, cheerful colours. Search for 'office', and Kuler returns colours found in most offices.

> ⚠ **ALERT:** You can always modify a chosen template or use a photograph to generate a colour combination. For instance, if I selected the 'death' palette, I would probably replace a grey colour with a deep, blood-red. If I wanted to use a photo, I would find one of a graveyard, or something equally spooky, and use it to generate my palette.

Accept that colour choices may not appear as you wish

Some systems and monitors are better than others. You must accept this fact and realise that your artistic creations might not always appear to your exact specification.

1 Navigate to the Name that Colour website (www.chir.ag/phernalia/name-that-color) and notice the sunset graphic. It uses subtle colour shading to great effect; it is just a slightly less great effect than that displayed on my Daewoo.

2 Here you can see my MacBook laptop's screen. The other image has been modified to resemble the graphic's appearance on my surplus Daewoo monitor that I got for free on CraigsList (www.craigslist.org).

3 On the Daewoo monitor, the colours aren't as brilliant and are slightly washed-out, and the subtle shading is slightly less subtle.

MacBook laptop screen

Daewoo monitor

? DID YOU KNOW?

As I write this book on my MacBook, my second display is a surplus Daewoo monitor. The monitor, compared to my brand new Apple MacBook's display, doesn't show colours as brightly and adds a subtle grey tint.

? DID YOU KNOW?

Monitors sometimes render colours incorrectly, and all your hard work getting an exact shade might be wasted effort. Before you design that perfect graphic, using colours such as Akaroa, Citrine White or Seashell Peach, realise that what you produce might be slightly off, depending upon a user's monitor.

Use text and background colour harmoniously

Make text and background colours work harmoniously together. Better yet, keep your background white or off white (I prefer whitesmoke) and your text black. Ensuring your colours have sufficient contrast keeps your site readable.

1 The first image shown here is a light gray background with dimgray text. Legible, but not optimal if the site is a text-heavy information site that readers go to for information.

2 The second image is a whitesmoke background with dimgray text. It is slightly easier to read and would probably be sufficient for most readers.

3 The third image is a whitesmoke background with black text. It's easy to read, but does not match the site's colours or style.

Although all three are suitable choices, my choice would be whitesmoke with a dimgray text for this site.

! ALERT: Remember your audience. If you are developing a site for older users whose eyesight may not be as good as it once was, you might strongly consider a white background with black text. People's ability to distinguish light shade differences tends to diminish with age.

? DID YOU KNOW?

Colours must have sufficient contrast between the background and text. Insufficient contrast makes your site unusable to some people, particularly those with diminished vision. A good rule is that if your site's text is illegible when viewed on a black and white monitor, you should change your background and foreground colour combination.

6 Texture

Introduction

Texture is the tactile quality of a visual design. On the Web, texture adds a third dimension to a two-dimensional canvas, the computer screen. You can use texture to make pages more visually appealing, set a mood, highlight a page's call to action, separate content into logical blocks, guide visitors' eyes to important content and navigational elements, and enhance brand identity.

One of the primary purposes of texture is to add depth to a two-dimensional design, but there are other ways of creating the illusion of depth, including the use of drop-shadows, gradients and overlapping objects. In this chapter, I show you how to use textures and other techniques to create tactile, three-dimensional designs that further your site's goals.

Add texture with a repeating pattern

A common way to add texture is to use a small repeating background image to create a textured pattern. Because the image is small, it loads quickly and does not negatively affect the site's performance.

1 Create or download a small image to use as your repeating background image. (The example shown here is from bgpatterns.com.)

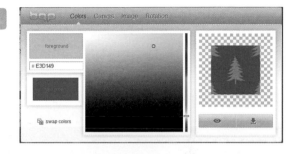

2 Create a CSS background-image style for the element behind which you want the background created, and include the CSS background-repeat property value, as in the following example:

```
body {background-image:url('ktwt4ew.png'); background-repeat:repeat; }
```

3 Notice how the image repeats vertically and horizontally to fill the space with a repeating pattern.

HOT TIP: You do not need to be an artist. Google 'background patterns' or 'background textures' to find small images that produce seamless patterns.

ALERT: Be careful not to use textures in a way that reduces the readability of the text on a page.

Add texture with a non-repeating image

A more sophisticated way to add texture is to use a photograph or textured graphic as a non-repeating background image.

1. Create or download a textured background image of the desired dimensions.

2. Create a CSS background-image style for the element behind which you want the background created; for example: body {background-image:url('grunge. jpg'); }

3. Notice that the image appears behind the page's content.

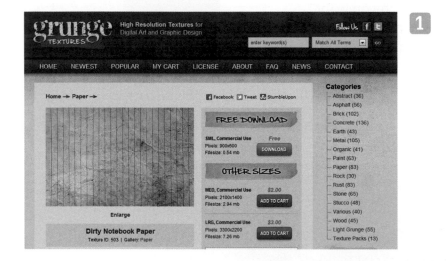

1

3

4 Consider dividing the graphic into three or more parts and having the middle section repeat vertically down the page. (This reduces the size of the graphic, while making it flexible enough to cover a page of any length.)

5 Notice the CSS template Lonelyness, which you can download from Open Source Web Design (www.oswd.org), pieces together five parts of a background image.

4

5

! **ALERT:** Make sure the background image is as wide as the page.

HOT TIP: If you divide the background graphic into three or more parts, the middle section can be a very thin sliver because it will repeat to fill the space.

HOT TIP: If you use multiple images in your site design, such as background images and buttons, consider using CSS sprites to combine the images. Creating and using CSS sprites is beyond the scope of this book, but you can Google 'how to use sprites' for details.

Use perspective for depth and to direct the eye

Perspective is another design technique that adds dimension and can be used subtly to guide the user through your content.

1 Download the Outside CSS template by styleshout.com. Notice the template follows good usability best practices by placing the logo on the upper left corner.

2 But notice the photograph. The fence line directs your eye away from the logo. A photograph usually draws a viewer's eye towards its centre. The eye then follows any strong lines in the photograph. The intersection of beach and sea draws the eye towards the logo, but the fence's pull overshadows the beach and sea intersection.

3 Notice the same template with the photo reversed. It draws the viewer's eye towards the logo.

HOT TIP: You can use textures to call attention to specific elements on a page – for example, by contrasting a bright, bold logo against a muted, textured background.

Use drop-shadows to add depth

Adding drop-shadows to images, boxes or text is a great way to create a sense of depth.

1 Add drop-shadows to images to create three-dimensional graphics.

2 Add drop-shadows to text in a graphics program or by using the CSS3 text-shadow property, such as h1 `{text-shadow: gray -2px 2px 5px; }`

3 Use the CSS3 box-shadow property to create a drop-shadow for boxed elements; for example: aside `{border: solid 1px; box-shadow: 10px 10px 10px #BBB; }`

ALERT: Only newer browsers support CSS3, and support for some CSS3 properties varies even among newer browsers. Search the Web for 'css3 browser compatibility' to find the latest information on browser support for CSS3, along with workarounds to make some CSS3 features compatible with different browsers.

ALERT: When creating images for use on your site, consider using reflections instead of drop-shadows. Reflections are more subtle and are more in vogue at the time of writing this book, although popularity can change over time.

Use gradients to fade colour in or out

Gradients fade a colour in and out from one point on the screen to another. For example, you can have a gradient that fades from almost transparent to very intense blue. You can add gradient backgrounds by gradating a background image or using CSS3.

1 Notice that all graphics programs have a feature to create gradients.

2 Use ColorZilla's Gradient Generator at www.colorzilla.com/gradient-editor to create a gradient and generate the CSS code for producing it.

3 Copy and paste the CSS into your site's CSS file.

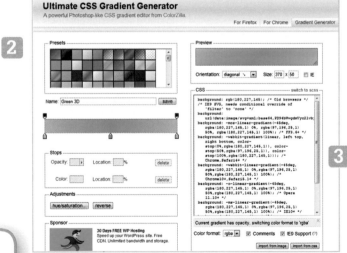

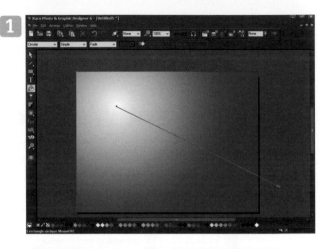

! ALERT: During the writing of this book, support for CSS3 gradients varied widely among browsers. Using a CSS3 gradient generator is the easiest way to ensure cross-browser compatibility, but older browsers will still be unable to display CSS3 gradients.

? DID YOU KNOW?

A background gradient is an excellent tool for highlighting the most important area of a page and directing the user's eyes.

Overlap objects for the illusion of three-dimensionality

One common way to create the illusion of three-dimensionality is to overlap objects on a page using CSS positioning. In the first example shown here, I created a header at bannerfans.com and then placed a clip art image from openclipart.org over it.

1. Use absolute positioning to specify the position of the upper left corner of each overlapping object.

2. Add the z-index property for each overlapping object to specify its position in the stack. The element with the highest z-index value appears on top.

```
#header {position:absolute; left:150px; top:80px; z-index: 0; }

#frog {position:absolute; left:50px; top:50px; z-index: 1; }
```

3. Use fixed positioning if you want the element to appear in a fixed position even when the user scrolls down the page.

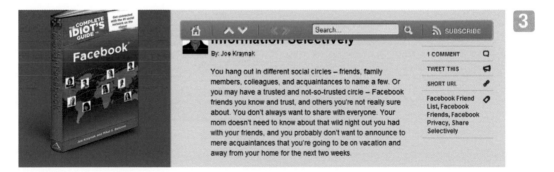

HOT TIP: Consider adding a drop-shadow to elements at or near the top of the stack to enhance the illusion of three-dimensionality.

HOT TIP: To produce an interesting visual effect, consider making elements at or near the top of the stack semi-transparent, so you can see the objects behind them. See the next section for details.

Use opacity/transparency for an interesting visual effect

Unless you specify otherwise, elements on a webpage are opaque; that is, you cannot see through them. In CSS3, you can use the opacity property to reduce an element's opacity and make it more transparent.

1 Use the opacity property to specify the desired opacity level: 0.0 for fully transparent (invisible) to 1.0 for fully opaque (cannot see through it).

2 Notice the differences in transparency when the opacity level of the box's background colour is adjusted.

ALERT: You can use CSS3 to make text and backgrounds transparent, but not images. If you want to make an image transparent, you need to do so in a graphics program and then save the image in a format that supports transparency, such as GIF.

ALERT: During the writing of this book, support for the CSS3 opacity property was fairly broad among newer web browsers, but you should test your site in the most popular browsers to ensure compatibility.

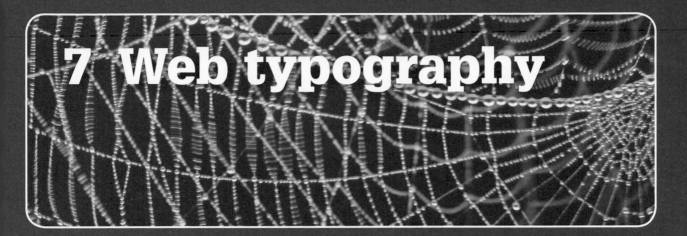

7 Web typography

Introduction

Typography is the art of choosing fonts and formatting text on a page so the page is visually pleasing and easy to read. Creating a webpage does not require an advanced proficiency with typography, but you should have a basic understanding of typography and of how to specify fonts and type size and apply other text enhancements. This chapter provides just that, by presenting several best practices. Following these best practices will make your content easier to read and more visually appealing.

Understand fonts

In pre-computer days, a font consisted of a family of print characters that shared the same typeface (design) and size. In the modern vernacular, 'font' is synonymous with 'typeface' and refers to font families like Arial, Courier or Times New Roman. You can adjust the size however you like and also apply 'enhancements', including colour, bold, italic and underline.

1 Notice the different Arial fonts and sizes shown here.

2 Fonts are divided into two major categories, serif and sans serif. Serif fonts add little strokes at letter ends while sans serif fonts do not.

3 You can also categorise fonts as monospaced or proportional. Proportional fonts give wider characters more room and narrower characters less and are easier to read. Monospace fonts are usually reserved for mathematical formulae, computer code and similar special text.

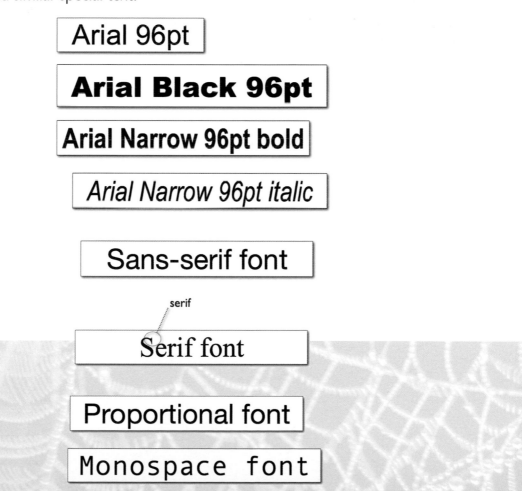

Arial 96pt

Arial Black 96pt

Arial Narrow 96pt bold

Arial Narrow 96pt italic

Sans-serif font

serif

Serif font

Proportional font

Monospace font

Specify the desired font

Unless you specify a font, each user's browser chooses one, which may ruin the appearance of your pages. When designing your website, you should specify your first choice font and additional fonts to use as backups if the font you specify is not installed on a particular user's computer.

1 Specify a font family for the body element using a style declaration like `body {font-family: Verdana, Georgia, Arial; }`

2 You can specify a different font family for different text elements within the body by adding a style declaration for each element like `h1 {font-family: 'Times New Roman';}`

3 Notice that the browser displays the text in the specified font, if that font is installed on the user's computer.

4 Notice that if a browser does not have access to the specified font, it uses a different font to display the text.

HOT TIP: In CSS3, you can upload a font family file to your web server and use @font-face to specify the location of the font, so any browser that accesses your site can display the font; for example:

```
@font-face {font-family:AwesomeFont; src:url('fonts/AwesomeFont.
tff'); }
```

Some older browsers may not support this CSS3 property.

WHAT DOES THIS MEAN?

Web-safe font: A font that is installed on most computer systems, including Windows and MacOS. Web-safe fonts include Arial, Arial Black, Courier New, Georgia, Lucida Console, Tahoma, Times New Roman and Verdana.

ALERT: Avoid the temptation to use numerous different fonts. In most cases, you want to use a single font for a consistent appearance throughout your site.

HOT TIP: Google provides a collection of hundreds of fonts that you can include in your design simply by adding an HTML link tag that specifies the location of that font on Google's web server. For details, visit www.google.com/webfonts. Also check out Typekit at typekit.com.

Specify relative font size or no size at all

Reading text on a monitor is difficult; do not make it more difficult by using small fonts. Even better, do not specify a font size. Instead, use a relative measurement, such as em or a percentage. Here Firefox allows setting the default font using the Preferences dialogue.

1 The hypothetical webpage here specifies its font as 12pt. When I change my browser's default font to Times 24pt, the page's fonts remain unchanged. Using a font size allows precise layout; however, it ignores a user's preferences. Ignoring a user's preferences is a bad thing; let the user specify his or her desired font size.

? DID YOU KNOW?

An em is the size of the letter 'm', so if in CSS you specified a text block was 2 em, you are essentially telling the browser to increase the text's size by twice the size of small m. Same with percentage: you increase or decrease the browser's default font by the percentage.

2 Now consider the second webpage, which specifies its font as 1.2 em. Now when I change my browser's default font to Times 20pt, the page's font size changes to reflect my preferred font size, as 1.2 em is relative to my preferred font size.

HOT TIP: Currently, it is trendy to specify small fonts. Many web designers adhering to the so-called Web 2.0 design fad specify text sizes smaller than the user's default font size. Resist this trend. If a user specifies his or her font as something outlandishly large, for instance Courier 24pt, it is your job to ensure your page displays well in the user's browser. Do not take the easy, but user unfriendly, shortcut and make the font smaller. Remember, the user might have a disability and be unable to read small fonts. I am very nearsighted, for instance, and I have difficulty reading fonts under 14pt on a computer screen. Do not make me squint to read your site – respect your users.

HOT TIP: Using a relative measure such as em or a percentage makes your webpage more accessible to users. Sight-impaired users can set their browser font large, and your site's fonts are displayed relative to the larger size.

ALERT: Resist the urge to control your page's font size. It is rude; it says to users, 'I don't care about your preferences.'

Increase line height to make text legible

Most people find reading single-spaced manuscripts difficult. Distinguishing between single-spaced sentences causes eyestrain. Now compound the inherent difficulties of reading text on a computer screen with the difficulties of reading single-spaced text, and the result is text which is virtually impossible to read.

1 Use the CSS line-height property to increase line height to 1.5 or 2; for example:

```
body {line-height: 2; }
```

2 Notice the difference in readability between single-spaced and double-spaced text.

HOT TIP: You can specify line height as a number, specific measurement (such as 12px) or relative amount (such as a percentage or a measurement in em). A number alone makes the space a multiple of the current font size, so if the font size is 16px and the line height is set to 2, the line height is 32px.

Left align text and headings in most situations

CSS enables text to be aligned left or right, or to be centred or justified (spread out evenly between the left and right margins). Unless you specify otherwise, all text is left-aligned, which makes sense because the beginning of each line is in a predictable location, so users do not have to search for it as they read from one line to the next. When designing pages, centre or right justify text only when you have good reason to do so.

1 Use the CSS text-align property to align text left or right, centre or justify; for example: `p {text-align: justify; }`

2 Use the CSS text-indent property to indent the first line of a paragraph; for example: `p {text-indent: 5em; }`

3 Notice the right-justified text shown here. The ragged left edges force your eyes to scan to find each line's beginning.

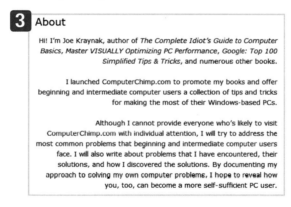

3 About

Hi! I'm Joe Kraynak, author of *The Complete Idiot's Guide to Computer Basics, Master VISUALLY Optimizing PC Performance, Google: Top 100 Simplified Tips & Tricks*, and numerous other books.

I launched ComputerChimp.com to promote my books and offer beginning and intermediate computer users a collection of tips and tricks for making the most of their Windows-based PCs.

Although I cannot provide everyone who's likely to visit ComputerChimp.com with individual attention, I will try to address the most common problems that beginning and intermediate computer users face. I will also write about problems that I have encountered, their solutions, and how I discovered the solutions. By documenting my approach to solving my own computer problems, I hope to reveal how you, too, can become a more self-sufficient PC user.

4 Look at the justified text. Justified text may be a little more difficult to read, but may be useful for short snippets of boxed text that is set apart from the main flow or for multi-column designs.

About

Hi! I'm Joe Kraynak, author of *The Complete Idiot's Guide to Computer Basics, Master VISUALLY Optimizing PC Performance, Google: Top 100 Simplified Tips & Tricks*, and numerous other books.

4 I launched ComputerChimp.com to promote my books and offer beginning and intermediate computer users a collection of tips and tricks for making the most of their Windows-based PCs.

Although I cannot provide everyone who's likely to visit ComputerChimp.com with individual attention, I will try to address the most common problems that beginning and intermediate computer users face. I will also write about problems that I have encountered, their solutions, and how I discovered the solutions. By documenting my approach to solving my own computer problems, I hope to reveal how you, too, can become a more self-sufficient PC user.

5 Look at the centred text. Centring large amounts of text is an obviously poor choice, as now both left and right edges are ragged.

About

Hi! I'm Joe Kraynak, author of *The Complete Idiot's Guide to Computer Basics, Master VISUALLY Optimizing PC Performance, Google: Top 100 Simplified Tips & Tricks*, and numerous other books.

I launched ComputerChimp.com to promote my books and offer beginning and intermediate computer users a collection of tips and tricks for making the most of their Windows-based PCs.

Although I cannot provide everyone who's likely to visit ComputerChimp.com with individual attention, I will try to address the most common problems that beginning and intermediate computer users face. I will also write about problems that I have encountered, their solutions, and how I discovered the solutions. By documenting my approach to solving my own computer problems, I hope to reveal how you, too, can become a more self-sufficient PC user.

6 Notice the left-aligned text. The lines are easy to read, as in a book.

About

Hi! I'm Joe Kraynak, author of *The Complete Idiot's Guide to Computer Basics, Master VISUALLY Optimizing PC Performance, Google: Top 100 Simplified Tips & Tricks*, and numerous other books.

I launched ComputerChimp.com to promote my books and offer beginning and intermediate computer users a collection of tips and tricks for making the most of their Windows-based PCs.

Although I cannot provide everyone who's likely to visit ComputerChimp.com with individual attention, I will try to address the most common problems that beginning and intermediate computer users face. I will also write about problems that I have encountered, their solutions, and how I discovered the solutions. By documenting my approach to solving my own computer problems, I hope to reveal how you, too, can become a more self-sufficient PC user.

HOT TIP: Centring typically works best for some, not all, headers, especially if your site has a header at the top of each page. You may also want to centre the footer.

HOT TIP: A centred header tends to look better if it is above justified text.

Make hyperlinks obvious

Web design used to have a strict rule about displaying links as blue, underlined text, which is how browsers display hyperlinks unless you specify otherwise. Now, however, that rule is not so strict. Feel free to change the appearance of hyperlinks, but use colour, underlining or other enhancements to clearly flag clickable text as hyperlinks.

1 Avoid underlining text that is not a link unless you have good reason to do so.

2 Use CSS to style the hyperlink element; for example:
```
a {color: red; text-decoration: underline; }
```

3 Notice that links are not blue and underlined here but are flagged with colour that conforms to the site's colour scheme.

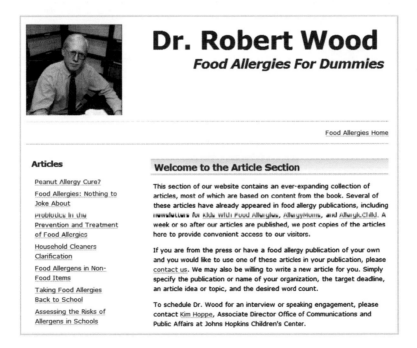

Place links as you would footnotes

Rather than interspersing your text with hyperlinks, try placing the links at your content's bottom, similar to footnotes. Be sparing when including links in your text, as hyperlinks reduce text legibility. The hyperlink looks different from its surrounding text. This difference forces a user's eye to slow down when scanning the text. The hyperlink is also distracting, as a user sees it is a hyperlink.

1 Review the hypothetical webpage here. It has hyperlinks scattered throughout the text.

SEE ALSO: Include links, especially links to other sites, sparingly, as explained in Chapter 2's 'Use external links sparingly and prudently'.

2 Now review the same page, with significantly fewer scattered hyperlinks. It has only a couple of text hyperlinks and includes the remainder below the content under a 'Further Reading' header, which makes it much more readable.

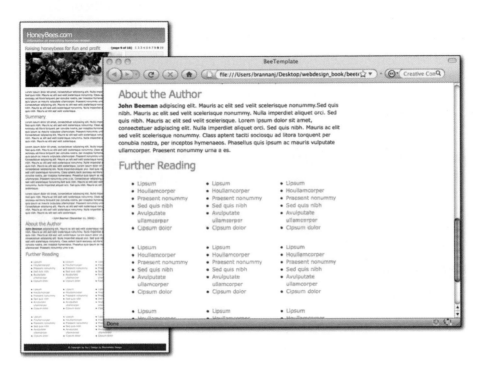

Avoid using ALL capital letters

Capitalising all letters in a word is usually bad practice for several reasons. Online it is the equivalent of shouting. In addition, it makes the text more difficult to read. If you need to emphasise text, use boldface or italics or increase the font size.

1 Notice the first page shown here. This page capitalises its headings.

2 The second page initial capitalises its headings.

3 The third page's headings capitalise only the first letter of the first word.

ALERT: Capitalising the first letter of each word in a heading is standard practice, but some styles call for capitalising only the first letter of the first word of a heading or title.

? DID YOU KNOW?
I based the hypothetical webpage used in this section on the Bitter Sweet CSS template by Arcsin.

Add sufficient padding around boxed text

If you use the CSS border property to display a box around text, make sure you have enough space between the box and its contents. You can add spaces using the CSS padding property.

1 When adding a border, add padding around text with the CSS padding property; for example: `article {border: solid 1px; padding: 4px; }`

2 Notice that a box's borders are usually too close to its contents.

3 Notice that the addition of padding makes the box and its contents appear more attractive.

> **HOT TIP:** For a more subtle presentation of boxed text, instead of using the CSS border property, use the background-colour property; for example: `aside {background-color: #F5F5F5; }`

2
Tip
To write clearer, more powerful prose, avoid the passive voice and weak sentence structures, such as those that begin with "There are..." and "It is..." Think *subject-verb*.

Also carefully consider the words you choose – your *diction*. Choosing precise words not only communicates more clearly but also adds variety.

3
Tip
To write clearer, more powerful prose, avoid the passive voice and weak sentence structures, such as those that begin with "There are..." and "It is..." Think *subject-verb*.

Also carefully consider the words you choose – your *diction*. Choosing precise words not only communicates more clearly but also adds variety.

? DID YOU KNOW?

The CSS box model enables you to create style declarations for several properties of a box:
- **Border:** Line thickness, style (solid, dotted, etc.), colour, and so on for the line that defines the box's perimeter.
- **Background:** The colour or image that appears behind the box's contents.
- **Padding:** The space between what's inside the box and the line that defines the border.
- **Margin:** The space between the box and what is outside it.
- **Outline:** A boundary outside the border used primarily to highlight an element.

8 Images

Introduction

A webpage without images is difficult to imagine. Images convey important information and, when used effectively, tend to make webpages more appealing. In this chapter you will explore several best practices for including images on your site. The chapter's purpose is to familiarise you enough with web graphics so you can effectively add them to your website, and have the graphics be relevant and visually pleasing.

Important: Manipulating images requires time and expertise. Unless you are adept at using graphics editing tools, obtaining the 'just-right' look can consume your time budget. Consider hiring an artist for any original artwork or designs.

Choose the right file format: JPEG, PNG, SVG or GIF

When creating or obtaining images to use on your website, choose the most appropriate graphics file format for each image: JPEG (Joint Photographers Expert Group), PNG (Portable Network Graphics), SVG (Scalable Vector Graphics) or GIF (Graphics Interchange Format).

1 Use JPEG for photographs and other images that have many colours and shades.

2 Use PNG for images created in most graphics programs.

HOT TIP: Use Flash instead of the GIF format to create animations.

3 Use SVG for icons, clip art, and other graphics you need to scale without any loss in resolution.

4 Use GIF only when necessary for small graphics that use basic colours.

Consider including a logo for brand identity

A logo is an image or stylised text that instantly identifies a business, organisation or product. Many sites repeat their logo in the same location on every page, typically in the upper left corner, to reinforce the site's brand identity. When designing websites, consider whether including a logo would help the site more effectively achieve its goal.

1 Visit popular sites.

2 Notice that most popular sites include a logo near the upper left corner.

3 Notice that although logos are typically simple, each has a unique appearance.

HOT TIP: Design simple logos with very basic colour schemes that symbolise the business, organisation or product you are trying to promote.

HOT TIP: You can find several tools on the Web for creating logos. Visit flamingtext.com for a few easy-to-use but powerful tools, including Logos and ImageBot.

SEE ALSO: An attractive colour or colour combination is important in the design of a logo. See Chapter 5, 'Using web colour effectively', for details.

Design an attractive header image

Although you can create a header for your site using HTML and CSS to display text against a colour background, most sites use a header image to add texture. You can create a header image using any number of graphics programs, such as Photoshop, or by using a free online tool, as shown here.

1 Go to www.bannerfans.com.

2 Choose a layout or upload an image of your own.

3 Click 'Text & Fonts' to enter your text and choose the desired font.

4 Use the other tabs to apply additional visual effects.

5 Choose the desired file format and download the header image for use on your site.

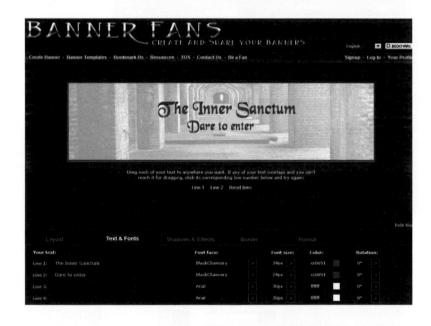

HOT TIP: When adding a header image, be sure to use HTML to make the header image clickable, so that when a user clicks the image your site's homepage appears.

SEE ALSO: You may want to use a header image along with other images to form a background for your web pages. See Chapter 6, 'Texture', for details. If your header contains text, as most do, see Chapter 7, 'Web typography', for more about what to consider when choosing fonts.

Use only relevant images

Before adding an image, ask yourself if the image is relevant to the page. If it is not relevant, do not include it. If choosing images for your header, choose images relevant to the entire site. If choosing images for content, choose images relevant to the content.

1 Choose a header image that is relevant to all content on the site.

2 Choose images that are relevant to the content on the site.

3 Notice that most of the images on this page are functional as well as visually appealing; for example, the image below 'Flights' is of an aeroplane.

HOT TIP: Using images as 'eye candy' to make a page appear more attractive than a text-only page is perfectly acceptable, but make the images functional as well as decorative by choosing images that fit with the theme of the page or website.

HOT TIP: When choosing images to promote a site's brand, make sure the images coordinate with the site's colour scheme. Use images with high-contrast colours to draw attention to a call to action, such as a new product announcement or the option to register.

Use images legally

When selecting images to use on your site, the safest option is to use images you have created or obtained permission directly from the creators to use. Simply copying images from websites is an open invitation for others to sue you for copyright violation.

If you simply must have an image, email the site's owner, find out the image's source and request permission to use the image from the person who owns it.

1 Purchase royalty-free stock images on sites like iStockPhoto.com. (Prices vary based on image, use and size/quality.)

ALERT: Beware of sites that offer free images and do not include licensing language or terms of use for those images. Legitimate sites typically specify how you are permitted to use the image and any attribution requirements.

HOT TIP: Several sites offer free images legitimately, including morgueFile.com, freestockphotos.com, openphoto.net and pdphoto.org. However, be sure to read and honour the licensing agreement for each photo. In many cases, to use a photo, you must add an attribution and link back to the creator's site.

ALERT: Royalty-free stock images are very affordable for web use, but costs rise for high-quality versions used for commercial purposes, such as for printing on T-shirts for sale. If you purchase rights for use on a single website, use the image only on a single website.

2 Browse images in Flickr's Creative Commons group.

3 Click the link under License to read the terms of use.

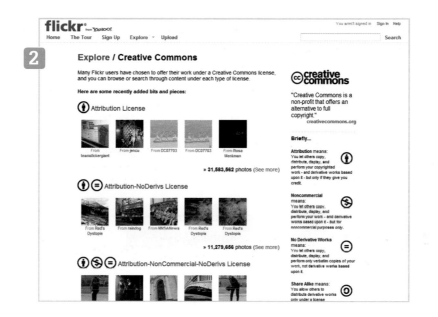

ALERT: A Creative Commons licensed photograph does not constitute a person's consent to be photographed. It applies only to copyright. If the photograph is in a public location, and you are using the photograph non-commercially, then you are probably fine, as a person cannot expect privacy in a public place. Nevertheless, if you use the photo commercially, you might be violating that person's rights. Consult a lawyer for guidance.

HOT TIP: Perform a Google Image Search and then choose the 'Advanced Search' option, scroll down the page and click 'Only images labelled for reuse', and then click 'Search Images'. The search results display images you can license by obtaining permission from their owners.

Use scalable vector graphics when possible

Scalable vector graphics (SVG) are compact, high-quality images that you can scale to any size without a loss in quality.

1 Visit openclipart.org for a large collection of free, public domain SVG clip art.

2 When previewing an image, click 'View Image' to display the SVG version.

3 Right-click the image, click 'Save as', and save the image to a folder on your computer's hard drive.

Crop your photos

Before uploading an image to the Web, crop it to remove unnecessary detail. Cropping creates a photo with a more precise message. Cropping also reduces a photo's dimensions, which results in a smaller file size that improves your site's performance.

1 Open the image you want to crop in an image editing program and use the File, Save as command to create a copy of the image, so you retain the original.

2 Notice the original image is 2048x1536 pixels and 613.6KB, much too large for a regular webpage with content.

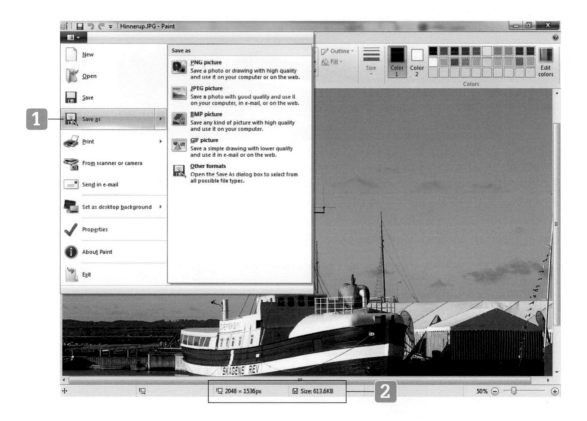

HOT TIP: Crop out as much extraneous detail in a photo before resizing it to retain as much detail as possible.

3 Reducing the dimensions to 410x308 pixels (20% of the original size) reduces the file size to 46.9KB, but notice the detail is lost. Instead crop the image, and then reduce its dimensions.

4 Crop the image first to reduce its dimensions to 1057x1385 and its size to 371.4KB. Then reduce the dimensions to 410x554. Cropping the image before reducing its dimensions results in a 85.2KB file size, and the image shows a larger version of the most important object – the boat.

Edit a photo before using it on a webpage

Before placing an image on your website, edit it for quality and size.

1 Open the photo in a photo editing program and use the 'Save As' command to save a copy of it under another name, so the original remains intact.

2 Use the photo editing program's features to adjust brightness, contrast, colour balance and other image attributes for optimum quality.

3 Adjust the size of the image with the aspect ratio locked to avoid distortion.

3

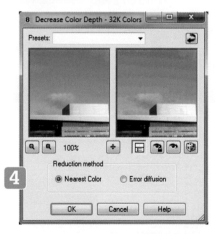

Resize	
Original Dimensions	
Width:	2048 Pixels (6.827 Inches)
Height:	1536 Pixels (5.120 Inches)
Resolution:	300.000 Pixels / Inch

Pixel Dimensions (22% x 22%)

Width: 450 — Pixels
Height: 338

Print Size

Width: 1.500 — Inches
Height: 1.125

Resolution: 300.000 — Pixels / Inch

☑ Resample using: Smart Size
☐ Maintain original print size
☑ Lock aspect ratio: 1.3333 to 1
☑ Resize all layers

OK Cancel Help

4 Experiment with JPEG file compression to reduce the file size as much as possible while retaining acceptable quality of appearance.

4

8 Decrease Color Depth - 32K Colors

Presets:

100%

Reduction method
◉ Nearest Color   ○ Error diffusion

OK   Cancel   Help

? DID YOU KNOW?
JPEG remains the preferred format for displaying photographs on the Web and often results in smaller file sizes for photographs. When creating images in a graphics program, however, the PNG format may result in smaller files.

! ALERT: Although you can reduce the dimensions and quality of an image to make smaller files that load faster, make reasonable adjustments so the drop in quality is not noticeable. A site that looks terrible is as likely to drive visitors away as one that loads slowly.

Use icons

Depending on the nature of your site, you may want to draw a distinction between clip art and icons and opt for using icons. The difference between the two is that clip art tends to appear cartoonish, which is inappropriate for most business and professional websites. Of course, if the site is designed for children or has a less serious tone, clip art may be more appropriate.

1 Review the sample of icons from Crystal Project. Notice the icons' consistent and professional appearance. I obtained these icons from the www.kde-look.org website. You can also obtain them from the creator's website: www.everaldo.com. The icons are licensed LGPL.

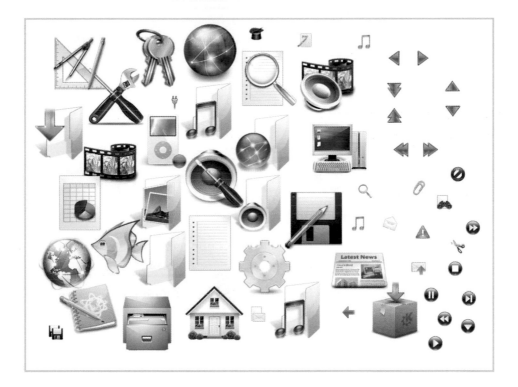

? DID YOU KNOW?

The kde-look.org website is part of opendesktop.org. A sister website is gnome-look.org, where you can also find high quality icons, such as the icon set Oxygen Refit 2.

! ALERT: If you use something licensed under GPL, you must make your site's code GPL. If something is licensed under LGPL, you can use it without opening the source code to your own extensions.

2 Navigate to www.kde-look.org and find the search form at the bottom of the ARTWORK menu on the page's left. Without entering anything, click 'Search'.

3 Click on the licence drop-down; notice you can limit your results by a work's licence. Search for Crystal Project, and you will find the icon theme.

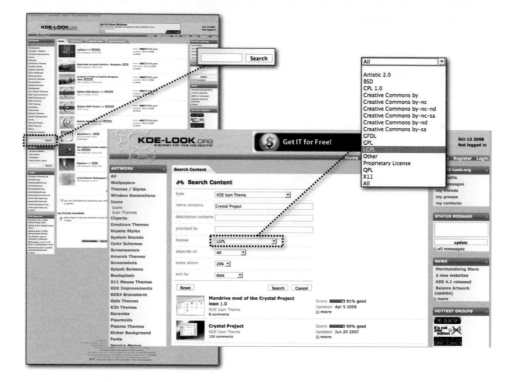

ALERT: If using KDE-Look to find icons or clip art, ensure the particular collection's licence is LGPL, or Creative Commons – Attribution. Alternatively, contact the creator to license the work.

HOT TIP: If choosing an icon collection, try using icons from the same collection. This helps your page maintain a consistent appearance.

ALERT: Do not use banner ad animation as a role model for including animated GIFs. Banner ads have one purpose: capturing your attention. The only thing an advertiser cares about is that you see their ad. So animated women dance next to promises to lower your mortgage interest rate, and cute jumping puppies sell web-hosting services. But the puppies and dancing girls are there solely to get your attention, not to make your browsing more aesthetic. Leave this nonsense to advertisers.

Use the alt attribute for images on your webpage

HTML documents include images using the <img> tag. Image tags have an attribute called alt, short for alternative, which provides alternative text if the image cannot be displayed. Ensure all images have an alt tag.

Here we can see Firefox displaying a page without graphics enabled.

HOT TIP: Visually impaired users rely upon screen readers for browsing websites. Screen readers read an image's alt attribute to the user. If you have no alt attribute, the user cannot access the image's content. If your site needs to be accessible to the visually impaired, always use the alt attribute for every image.

Consider using thumbnails if appropriate

If your site displays a considerable number of photographs, or needs a detailed graphic to illustrate a concept, consider using thumbnails. A thumbnail is a smaller, lower quality image displayed instead of the original. A hyperlink is added to the thumbnail so that when clicked, the original is displayed. By providing a thumbnail, you do not needlessly consume bandwidth with photographs a user might not want to view.

1 Consider this hypothetical webpage, which is a simple photograph album page created using Apple's iWeb. The page displays thumbnails of the photographs I added. By displaying the thumbnails, a user's browser must only load the thumbnails.

2 Upon clicking the photograph, the page replaces the thumbnail with the larger, more detailed photograph.

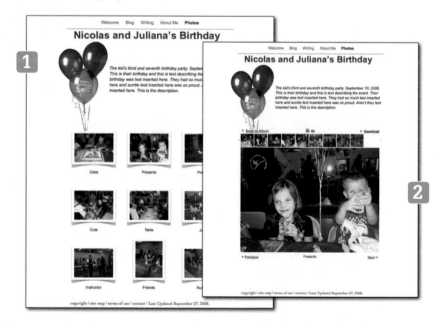

ALERT: Note, do not use hot-linking when using thumbnails. Creating a thumbnail of an image and placing the thumbnail on your website but linking to the original larger image on someone else's site is bandwidth theft and probably copyright violation.

9 Using multimedia effectively

Introduction

Multimedia is the use of more than one type of content, which may include text, images, audio, video and animation. If you search Google for a recent big budget movie, you are likely to find that the official movie site delivers an impressive multimedia experience, complete with movie trailers, on-location photos, downloadable wallpaper, interactive games and more. These big budget sites are typically designed in Flash, which is something I do not recommend for most organisations or individuals with more modest multimedia needs. Visitors are usually better served by a more basic site that includes multimedia elements where appropriate. In this chapter I provide guidance on best practices related to multimedia, so you can design sites that serve the visitors' needs without overwhelming them with distracting, over-the-top content.

Leverage the power of YouTube

An easy and free way you can add multimedia to your site is by embedding YouTube video on webpages or in blog posts. All you do is upload your video to YouTube and then copy and paste an HTML tag in the source code for a page or post. YouTube stores the video and plays it, incurring both the storage and the delivery costs.

1 Create a YouTube account, if you do not already have one, and log in to your account.

2 Click the 'Upload' link and follow YouTube's instructions to upload your video.

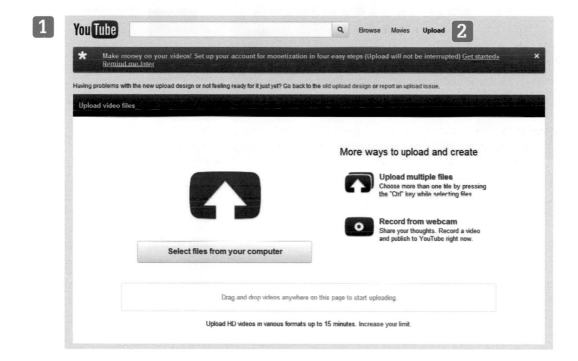

ALERT: Share other people's videos only with their express, written permission. The same copyright rules that apply to images (see Chapter 8) apply to video.

HOT TIP: YouTube enables you to specify the dimensions of the frame in which the video plays on your site, where the video playback starts (for example, 30 seconds into the video) and more. Search YouTube's Help system for 'embed' for additional details.

3 Display the video, click the 'Share' button and copy the desired source code for displaying the video on your site. (You may have the option of using a simple URL with the HTML5 <video> tag or using an HTML embed code for displaying the video on a frame, as shown here.)

4 Paste the code you copied into the HTML source code for the webpage or blog post wherever you want the video to appear.

HOT TIP: HTML5 includes a <video> tag that enables you to insert a video simply by specifying its location, but browser support for the video tag and the video file formats that browsers support vary. When supported, it will allow you to insert a video as easily as you insert an image, and the tag will look something like this:

```
<video src='video/sample-video.webm' width='640px' height='480px'
controls=controls> </video>
```

Understand the basics of video file formats and codecs

If you embed video using YouTube, most browsers will be able to play it. If you want to share video without YouTube, you need to know a little about video file formats and video codecs (coders/decoders) to ensure that most browsers will be able to play the video. For a browser to play a video, it must support both the video's file format and its codec.

1 Notice that video file formats include .mp4, .mov, .avi, .flv, .ogv and .webm. When you save a video file, the video program saves the video in a certain file format or prompts you to choose a format.

2 Notice that video codecs include MPEG-4, H.264, Sorenson Spark, Theora and H.264. The codec is the technology used to compress and decompress the video.

3 When saving and encoding files, use common formats with standard codecs, such as MPEG-4 or H.264 for .mp4 video, H.264 or Sorenson Spark for .flv video, Theora for .ogv video and vp8 for .webm video.

3

Production Preset Wizard

Create a Production Preset
Set the Production Preset name, description, and output format using the boxes below.

Preset name: Web Output
Description:

File format
- MP4/FLV/SWF - Flash outputs
- WMV - Windows Media video
- MOV - QuickTime movie
- AVI - Audio Video Interleave video file
- M4V - iPod, iPhone, iTunes compatible video format
- MP3 - audio only
- RM - RealMedia streaming video
- CAMV - Camtasia for RealPlayer streaming video
- GIF - animation file

Additional output options
- Create MP3 file   22.050kHz, Mono, 96kBits/sec
- Create M4V file   iPod High (320x240)

Description
MP4/SWF is the recommended format for online viewing. This format is compatible on multiple browsers including Windows, Mac, and Linux. MP4/SWF delivers high quality video at a small file size.

< Back   Next >   Cancel   Help

4 To ensure that your video plays in most browsers, include the video in several different file formats and specify those files using the <video>, <embed> and <object> tags.

4

```
<video width='640px' height='480px' controls='controls'>

<source src='movie.mp4' type='video/mp4' />

<source src='movie.ogg' type='video/ogg' />

<source src='movie.webm' type='video/webm' />

<object data='movie.mp4' width='640' height='480'>

<embed src='movie.swf' width='640' height='480'>

Your browser does not support video, <a href='movie.swf'>Click to save

or play video using a video player on your computer</a>

</embed>

</object>

</video>
```

HOT TIP: If you do not have a program that converts video to a format you need, search the Web for video format converters.

HOT TIP: For more about the Google sponsored webm video, visit www.webmproject.org.

Consider podcasting to deliver your multimedia

Have you ever wanted to do your own radio or television show? You can by podcasting. Podcasting, a term coined by combining iPod and broadcasting, is a common way to deliver video and audio over the Internet. The way it works is you create a video or audio show, and save it using a common audio or video format. You also create an XML file to describe the show and then upload both to a web server.

1 Record the podcast to digital format such as MP3 or MP4.

2 Create an RSS feed which describes your podcast.

3 Create a link on your website so users can listen to your podcast. This link points to the podcast. Create another link to the RSS feed so users can subscribe to your podcast.

4 Next time you record a new podcast you replace the RSS feed. Subscribed users are automatically notified of the change and can download the new episode.

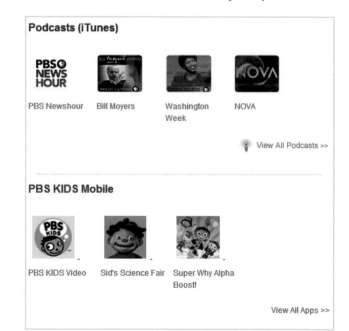

? DID YOU KNOW?

The steps for creating and posting a podcast vary depending on the tools you use. You may use your own audio or video recording software and create the source code for the feed manually, or use any of several online podcasting services to record, upload and create the feed.

🔥 HOT TIP: An easy way to set up a podcast is to use a podcast plugin for your content management system (CMS). For example, if you use WordPress to manage your website/blog, you can install a plugin like Buzzsprout Podcasting to eliminate some of the technical challenges. An added benefit of podcasting on a blog is that you can add more text to describe the podcast, which enables search engines to more effectively index your podcasts.

Consider linking to media files

You can embed video and sound in a webpage using the <video> or <embed> and <object> tags. But different browsers handle the multimedia differently. You must also size the content correctly, and the browser must have the appropriate plugin to handle the content. An easier way to include multimedia in your webpage is by linking to it. With a link, each browser selects the appropriate plugin or external application to play the media. If a browser does not know how to play the content, it prompts the user to save the media or select a program that should handle the media.

1 Consider the hypothetical webpage here. Along the page's left side are thumbnails of previous events by the fictional company. Each thumbnail is a link to its associated video.

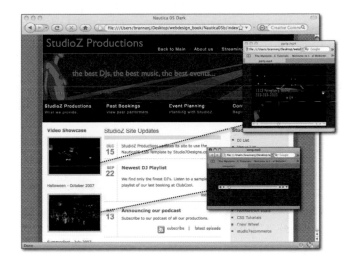

2 Upon clicking the top thumbnail, because the hyperlink has a target attribute with _blank as its value, the video opens in a new window. Safari loads the Quicktime plugin automatically and begins playing the video.

3 Upon clicking the link to the sample DJ music set, the MP3 file opens in a new window and Quicktime automatically begins playing the song.

> **HOT TIP:** In the multimedia link's HTML tag, include `target=" _ blank"`. A target with the _blank value plays in its own new tab or window.

> **ALERT:** Storing and delivering multimedia can be expensive. Videos are large, requiring ample disk space and bandwidth for your users to download the video. Either you host your own web server or, more likely, you pay someone to host your site. How much you pay depends upon your site's storage and bandwidth requirements. Including video content requires ample storage space and bandwidth. Have you ever seen the message 'bandwidth limit exceeded'? This is because someone has used too much bandwidth and must increase his or her service level. Increasing a service level costs money.

Include audio on your webpages

Many sites enable users to play audio clips, which may include voice narration, recorded music or sound effects. When adding audio to webpages, you run into many of the same problems as you do with video; that is, support for various HTML tags and video file formats and codecs vary among web browsers, so you have several options to consider.

1 Include a link users can click to play the audio with a JavaScript tag after the closing </body> tag that enables the Yahoo! Media Player to play the audio, as in the following example:

```
<a href="audio/music01.mp3">Play Music</a>

<script type="text/javascript" src="http://mediaplayer.yahoo.com/
js"></script>
```

ALERT: Make audio on-demand, so it plays only if the user chooses to listen. Use the HTML5 <audio> tag or older HTML <embed> and <object> tags to play audio automatically in the background only if doing so makes sense and enhances the site. In most cases, background audio is more annoying than useful.

2 Include the HTML <audio> and <embed> tags to play the audio in newer and older browsers.

3 Include a link users can click to play the audio on whichever audio player is set up to play files of that format on their computer, as in the following example:

```
<a href="audio/music01.mp3">Play Music</a>
```

If the user has no program installed that can play the file, the computer will display a prompt for the user to choose a program or save the file to play later.

2
```
<audio controls="controls" height="50px" width="100px">

<source src="audio/music.mp3" type="audio/mpeg" />

<source src="audio/music.ogg" type="audio/ogg" />

<embed height="50px" width="100px" src="audio/music.mp3" />

</audio>
```

HOT TIP: Like Yahoo!, Google has a player that you can embed on a webpage. To do so, include something like the following in your webpage source code:

```
<a href="audio/music.mp3">Play Song</a>
<embed type="application/x-shockwave-flash" wmode="transparent"
src="http://www.google.com/reader/ui/3523697345-audio-player.
swf?audioUrl=song.mp3" height="27" width="320"></embed>
```

Use Flash sparingly

Avoid excessive Flash animation. Just because an animation is Flash, and not an animated GIF, does not mean the animation is somehow better than an animated GIF.

1 Refer to the Flash template shown opposite: interesting, but not usable. To get the full effect, you must view it in a web browser. However, just by looking at it, you should realise this template, albeit cool, is unusable.

2 The next one, also graphically dazzling, does not label any links, and requires you to click on animated circles that constantly move, making navigation extremely difficult.

3 Both these templates are brilliant Flash design, and I definitely could not do better; but they are not usable.

4 If you are an artist, a photographer for example, then highlighting your art using a Flash template might be appropriate. For instance, consider the Flash template in the final pair. This shows a Flash template for a hypothetical photographer's site. It allows the photographer to display his or her photographs.

5 The photography website is also usable and presents the photographer's information clearly. The site's main links are along the bottom and if a user wishes to contact the artist, he or she could quite easily.

HOT TIP: If you learn nothing else from this book, remember that users will go to your site to fulfil a need. You usually fulfil needs with services, not amazing graphics.

HOT TIP: Designing an entire site in Flash is usually bad for search engine optimisation (SEO), because search engines cannot index Flash as easily as HTML text and tags.

? DID YOU KNOW?

A recent trend in web development is something called Rich Internet Applications (RIA). In an RIA, substantial portions of the Internet application functions in a user's browser. For instance, the application used in Chapter 5, Adobe Kuler, is a rich Internet application. To load and use the application in your browser, you must have the latest Flash plugin installed.

? DID YOU KNOW?

Before emulating an RIA such as Kuler, you should ascertain whether it is necessary. Kuler is an application which happens to be delivered by the Web; Kuler is not gratuitous special effects delivered using Flash. If you are delivering an application via the Web, consider an RIA. But if you simply want to use an RIA's cool features to create impressive navigation, animation and other special effects, reconsider.

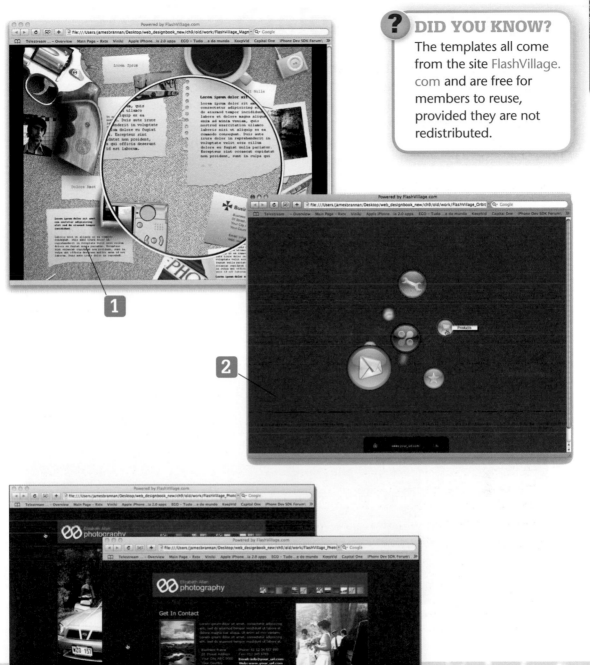

DID YOU KNOW?

The templates all come from the site FlashVillage. com and are free for members to reuse, provided they are not redistributed.

Avoid Flash splash screens

Splash screens are introductory pages that are typically highly stylised, animated and designed to impress. However, when most users, especially frequent visitors, visit a site and encounter a splash screen, they see it as an annoying obstacle and look for a quick way to get past it. As a web designer, you should be as eager to avoid splash screens as users are. Use splash screens only if you are certain they make sense and enhance the site. If you have any doubt, avoid them.

1 Look at the Flash splash animation shown here.

2 Notice the option to skip the splash screen in the lower right corner. If you simply must have a cool splash screen, provide an option for users who do not have Flash, or do not wish to experience your brilliance. Provide a link just below the animation to skip the splash screen.

? DID YOU KNOW?

User-test any splash screen before employing it. If you see that users quickly skip the splash screen, get rid of it.

HOT TIP: Introductory splash screens with dazzling animations usually impress only other designers and clients. Everyone else is likely to find them annoying.

10 Testing your website

Introduction

After planning and developing your site, test it. Testing is as important as design and development. Testing ensures that what you designed and developed actually works. And testing should be thorough; you can consider your site tested only after you have made sure it functions correctly, is usable and offers the functionality you envisioned it having.

Troubleshoot appearance issues

When you are composing pages in HTML and CSS, appearance issues are likely to arise. Perhaps the header has too much white space above or below it, text does not align as you had intended it to or certain colours look odd. Inspecting the code to identify problems is often time consuming and frustrating, so use a tool like Firebug for Mozilla Firefox to help troubleshoot problems.

1. Download and install Mozilla Firefox from mozilla.com/firefox.

2. Go to addons.mozilla.org, search for 'firebug', mouse over the Firebug entry and click 'Add to Firefox'. (Restart Firefox after installing Firebug.)

3. In Firefox, open the webpage you want to inspect.

4. Click 'Inspect Element'.

5. Click the element you want to inspect. Firebug displays the element's HTML and CSS.

6. Edit the CSS in the preview window to experiment with different fixes without actually changing the CSS for the page. (You can edit the actual CSS later after locating the problem.)

HOT TIP: Numerous addons are available for Mozilla Firefox and are specifically designed to help with webpage design and development. I encourage you to browse the collection of addons.

HOT TIP: Google Chrome supports extensions for web developers. Go to chrome.google.com/webstore, click 'Extensions', click 'Developer Tools', and browse the collection. Other browsers, including Internet Explorer and Apple Safari, have built-in tools or addons for developers. Search your browser's Help system and the Web to find out what is available.

Check for broken links and missing content

Two problems that are guaranteed to drive traffic from your site are broken links and missing content. With a broken link, the user clicks the link only to be greeted by an error message. With missing content, the browser displays an error icon in place of a missing image or video, or a user clicks a link and finds a blank page or error message. To avoid disappointing and frustrating users, check for broken links and missing content.

1 Click every button and every link to make sure it displays the intended destination page.

2 Check every page for missing media called for by \<img\>, \<video\> and other tags.

3 Make sure all media files play as you intended them to.

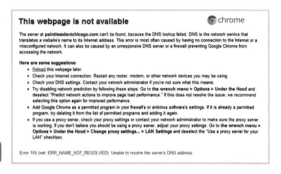

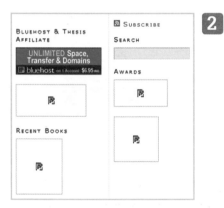

HOT TIP: If a page is loaded with links, consider using the W3C Link Checker to validate them. Go to validator.w3.org/checklink, click in the Address box, type or paste the address of the page you want to check and click 'Check'. Link Checker displays a report indicating any problems.

ALERT: Read every page from top to bottom, taking note of any errors in spelling or grammar. Better yet, have someone else proofread the site for you, test all links and buttons and report any errors. Sometimes having a fresh pair of eyes examine the site helps rid the site of errors.

Test using more than one browser

Websites and webpages often appear and perform differently in different browsers. Test your site in at least the four leading web browsers: Firefox, Internet Explorer, Safari and Google Chrome. Depending upon your target audience and resources, you might also test in older browser versions and on mobile devices, such as iPhones.

1 Display each page in the four leading web browsers.

2 Carefully inspect each page for differences. In the example shown here, the CSS text drop-shadow appears in Google Chrome but not when displayed in Internet Explorer.

HOT TIP: Certain services on the Web enable you to view your website in several different browser versions. Consider Browser Shots at browsershots. org, Spoon Browser Sandbox at spoon.net/browsers, and BrowserSeal at browserseal.com.

ALERT: When you do not specify what you want in your HTML and CSS, the browser renders the page according to its own internal settings, which vary among browsers and even among different versions of the same browser. Remember, always test in different browsers.

ALERT: You may also want to test your website in smartphone simulators (also called emulators). Search the Web for 'smartphone emulators' to find emulators that run on webpages or that you can install on your computer.

Test your site's usability

Always test that users can use your site. If you have a large budget, you can hire users to test your site. If the site is a personal site, get friends and family or colleagues to test. Ensure the testers were not involved in the site's development though, so you can get unbiased feedback.

1 Refer to the Flash template shown here.

2 Consider its usability. Consider the links – for instance, how would a user know which link points to the 'client history' information?

3 After blindly clicking, you eventually find the link. You could make the site more usable by labelling the hyperlinks, even if they do detract from the site's ambiance. At least provide a mouse-over tooltip that identifies the link's target when a user moves their cursor over the eye.

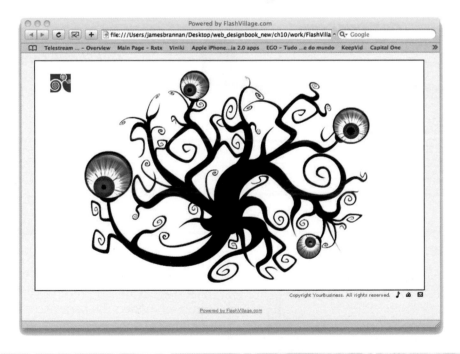

HOT TIP: Do not have testers clicking blindly. Get testers to perform scripted tasks. Can the user perform the task quickly and easily? If not, consider changing your site. A hard to use task is usually an unperformed task.

HOT TIP: Observe users as they perform assigned tasks, if possible. You may observe someone having great difficulty performing a task who tells you the task was easy.

4 Navigate to the 'client history' page. Now consider how to return to the main menu. There are no apparent links. Intuition tells me to click on the eye again; however, you should not force users into relying upon intuition. Clearly label your links.

5 Look again at the homepage. Who is the website for? What is the website about? Nothing on the homepage answers these questions except for the small copyright statement at the page's lower right.

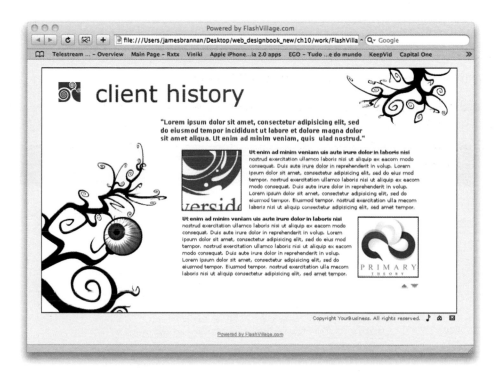

HOT TIP: If you wait until your site is complete, usability testing might provide you with a nasty surprise. Your site might be unusable, and a fully developed site is much harder to modify than a prototype site. You might consider usability testing when you have a prototype navigation template rather than waiting until completely developing the site. Test early and test often.

Check for accessibility issues

All websites should be accessible to all users regardless of their abilities and disabilities. If a user is visually impaired, for example, having text descriptions of images and scripts for any video that includes narration helps these users access the same information in a different form.

1 Run your web browser and access the Functional Accessibility Evaluator at fae.cita.uiuc.edu.

2 Enter the address of the page you want to evaluate and click 'Evaluate'.

3 Review the Summary Report for any issues you need to address.

---

fae   **Functional Accessibility Evaluator 1.1**
University of Illinois at Urbana-Champaign

About FAE | Register | Log In

Run FAE

Summary Report
Page Report

Summary Report

Untitled Report	2012-02-29 13:38
Ruleset: 1011-1 (current)	
URL: http://www.pearsoned.co.uk/	

Evaluation Results by Best Practices Main Category

Category	Status [1]	% Pass	% Warn	% Fail
Navigation & Orientation	Almost Complete	88	7	3
Text Equivalents	Almost Complete	75	25	0
Scripting	Complete	100	0	0
Styling	Almost Complete	83	16	0
HTML Standards	Complete	100	0	0

Note: % Pass includes N/A results.

Evaluation Results by Best Practices Subcategory

Category/Subcategory	% Pass	% Warn	% Fail
Navigation & Orientation			
Titles (title & h1)	85	14	0
Subheadings (h2..h6)	100	0	0
Navigation Bars	66	33	0
Form Control Labels	100	0	0
Data Tables	100	0	0
Default Language	0	0	100

🔥 **HOT TIP:** Other accessibility evaluation tools are available, including the Web Accessibility Evaluation Tool at wave.webaim.org and HERA at sidar.org.

🔥 **HOT TIP:** You can review the W3C Content Accessibility Guidelines at www.w3.org/TR/WCAG10.

Evaluate your site's effectiveness in achieving its goals

Ensuring your site is accessible and usable is only part of testing. As important is that your site performs the functions it was intended to perform.

1 Refer to the Bodybuilding webpage in Chapter 1 (page 28). Notice that the site provides plenty of content that is valuable for the targeted audience/market.

2 Refer to your list of site requirements from Chapter 1 (page 30) and your use case diagram (page 31) to recall your site's goals.

3 Refer to the diagrams in Chapter 2 (pages 36 and 37). The first is an outline of the site built in later sections of Chapter 2. The second is the site map. Both diagrams provide good documents to check against the built site that follows on pages 53–56.

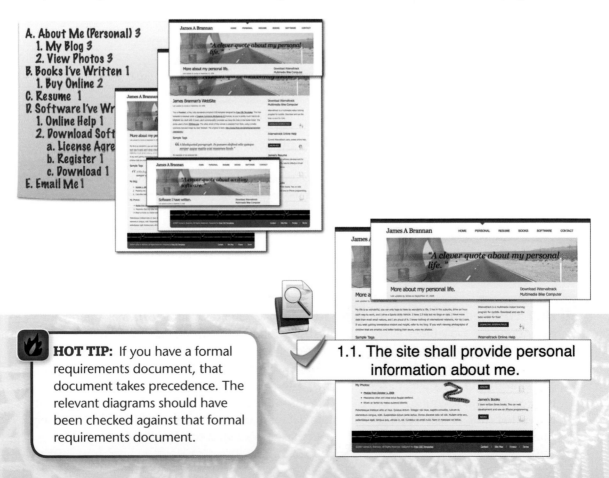

1.1. The site shall provide personal information about me.

HOT TIP: If you have a formal requirements document, that document takes precedence. The relevant diagrams should have been checked against that formal requirements document.

Test your site's speed

In the on-demand world of the Web, users are not accustomed to waiting. If your pages take more than a few seconds to load, users are likely to go elsewhere to have their needs met and their curiosities fed. Test your site's speed and compare it to competing websites to ensure that your site is at least as fast as the competition.

1 Open your web browser and go to developers.google.com/pagespeed.

2 Type the address of the webpage you want to test and click 'ANALYZE'.

3 Notice the page speed score.

4 Click an item on the left to find out more about an issue that you may want to address to improve performance.

HOT TIP: Addons or extensions are available for many of the leading browsers, including Firefox and Chrome, to evaluate page speed and identify issues that may be slowing down page load times.

HOT TIP: If you are building and managing your website using a content management system, such as WordPress, consider installing a page-caching plugin. Content management systems 'assemble' pages from a database. Caching saves a copy of a pre-assembled page, so when a browser requests it the database does not need to assemble it. Caching can make pages load considerably faster.

Deal with browser compatibility issues

A major challenge in web design is that web browsers adhere to no uniform standards, especially standards that relate to newer features such as those introduced in HTML5 and CSS3. You can avoid many issues by sticking with the basics, but sometimes basic makes a site appear boring or out of date. Here, I present some solutions that will require additional research on your part to implement.

1 Enable Google Chrome Frame for Internet Explorer by adding the following <meta> tag to all of the pages on your website:

```
<meta http-equiv="X-UA-Compatible" content="chrome=1">
```

2 Add the HTML5 JavaScript shiv code before the <body> tag on each page to have Internet Explorer recognise HTML5 elements:

```
<!--[if lt IE 9]>

<script src="//html5shiv.googlecode.com/svn/trunk/html5.js"></script>

<![endif]-->
```

3 Use browser prefixes (-moz- for Mozilla Firefox, -webkit- for WebKit browsers including Safari and Chrome, and -o- for Opera), when necessary, to specify browser support for various CSS properties.

4 Use Internet Explorer filters where necessary.

5 Use conditional CSS statements to target formatting for specific browsers.

6 Use browser and feature detection to automatically determine what a browser supports and specify HTML and formatting for that browser.

ALERT: Cross-browser compatibility is an evolving issue with evolving solutions. The solutions presented here only serve to remind you that solutions exist. Research the Web for the most current solutions.

1

```
<meta http-equiv="X-UA-Compatible" content="chrome=1">
```

2

```
<!--[if lt IE 9]>

<script src="//html5shiv.googlecode.com/svn/trunk/html5.js"></script>

<![endif]-->
```

3

```
aside {

border-radius: 5px;

-moz-border-radius: 5px;

-webkit-border-radius: 5px;

-o-border-radius: 5px; }
```

4

```
h1 { text-shadow: gray -2px 2px 5px;
filter: progid:DXImageTransform.Microsoft.Shadow ( direction=210,strength=
5,color='gray') ; }
```

5

```
.box { width: 490px; padding 5px; }

[if IE] .box { width: 500px; padding 10px; }
```

? DID YOU KNOW?

Internet Explorer is notorious for not conforming to standards. Google Chrome and Safari, both WebKit browsers, are generally considered the best in supporting standards. Google Chrome Frame essentially makes Internet Explorer act like a WebKit browser, but users must agree, when prompted, to allow it to be installed in their Internet Explorer browser.

Audit your site for SEO

Although web design tends to focus on appearance, you want users to be able to discover your site when they search for content the site provides, so test your site for search engine optimisation (SEO) and make as many adjustments as possible to optimise your site. The page here shows the SeoQuake addon for Firefox in action.

1 Run Firefox, go to addons.mozilla.org, search for 'seoquake', mouse over the SeoQuake entry and click 'Add to Firefox'. (Restart Firefox after installing SeoQuake.)

2 In Firefox, open the webpage you want to audit.

3 Click the 'Info' button in the SeoQuake toolbar.

4 Examine the page info, parameters and keyword density information.

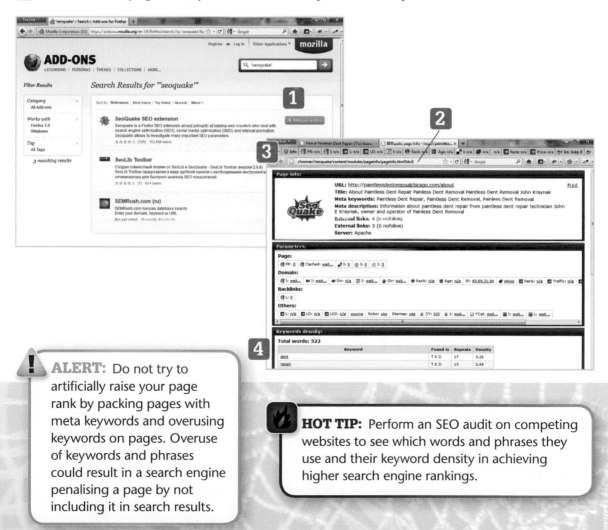

ALERT: Do not try to artificially raise your page rank by packing pages with meta keywords and overusing keywords on pages. Overuse of keywords and phrases could result in a search engine penalising a page by not including it in search results.

HOT TIP: Perform an SEO audit on competing websites to see which words and phrases they use and their keyword density in achieving higher search engine rankings.

Test your site using Google Webmaster Tools

Google features numerous tools to help webmasters improve site performance and SEO and identify issues that need to be addressed. Some issues that Webmaster Tools highlight may negatively affect your site's search engine ranking, so adding a site to Webmaster Tools and checking for problems is a good idea.

1 Create a Google account if you have not done so already and log in.

2 Go to www.google.com/webmasters/tools.

3 Click 'ADD A SITE', enter the URL of the site, click 'Continue', and follow the onscreen instructions to complete the process.

4 Return to the Webmaster Tools dashboard and click the site's name, if necessary.

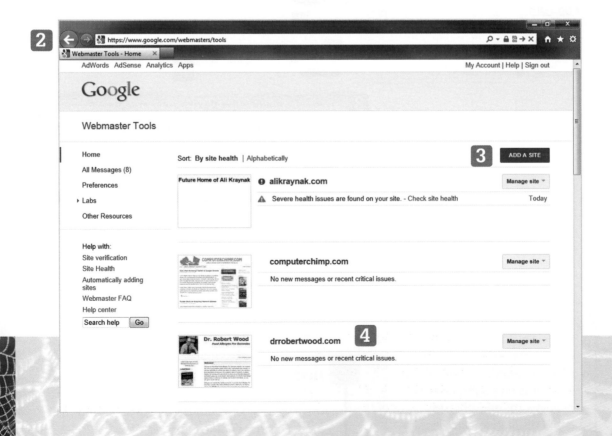

5 Explore the dashboard for signs of any problems, and address them.

Google

Webmaster Tools

drrobertwood.com ▾

Dashboard		
Messages		
▸ Site configuration		
▸ Your site on the web		
▸ +1 Metrics		
▸ Diagnostics		
▸ Labs		
Other Resources		

Help with:
Crawl errors
Search queries
Links to your site
About Sitemaps
Additional support
Help center

[Search help] [Go]

Search queries

Query	Impressions	Clicks
medical diagnosis	320	<10
dr wood	320	<10
food allergies	320	<10
dr. wood	170	<10
allergic reaction to food	170	<10
food allergy	170	<10
naet testing	170	<10
robert wood	110	<10
food allergic reactions	110	<10
rast panel	110	<10

Jan 27, 2012 to Feb 26, 2012

More »

Links to your site

Domains	Total links

Crawl errors

Restricted by robots.txt	20
Unreachable	26

Updated Feb 29, 2012

More »

Keywords

food (2 variants)
allergy (3 variants)
test (4 variants)
reaction (5 variants)
allergist (3 variants)

More »

Sitemaps

Sitemap	Status	URLs in web index
/sitemap.xml		32

More »

5

⚠ **ALERT:** Two things you want to attend to immediately are posting a site map and robots.txt file that tell search engines which content to index and not index on your site. If you use a content management system (CMS), such as WordPress, to manage your site, you can obtain plugins to generate a site map and robots.txt file and keep them up to date.

🔥 **HOT TIP:** Another tool that is helpful for tracking traffic to your website is Google Analytics. For details, visit www.google.com/analytics.

Validate your site's pages using the W3C's HTML Validator

Historically, HTML was not standardised. Different browsers added different features in an endless quest for web dominance. Netscape would add something brilliant, and the next Internet Explorer version would equal Netscape's brilliant feature, but add something even more brilliant. For several years, it was a browser arms race. The computer industry formed the W3C to standardise HTML, and browsers have been gravitating towards meeting the W3C's stricter standards. You should do the same. You can test whether your website's HTML syntax is correct using the W3C's HTML validation service.

1 Go to validator.w3.org.

2 Click in the Address box and type or paste the address of the page you want to validate.

3 Click 'Check'.

4 Review and correct any errors that the Validator identifies.

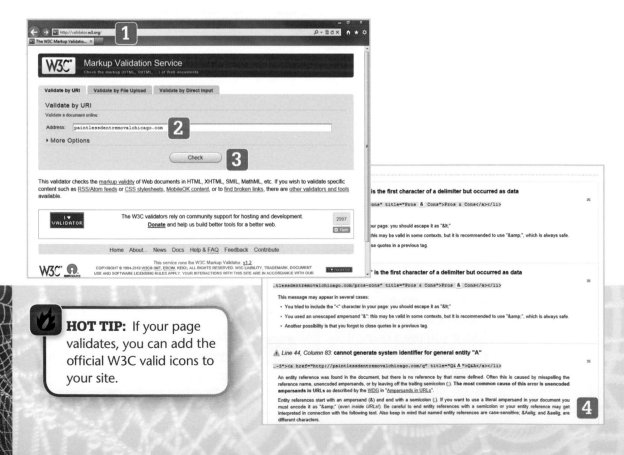

HOT TIP: If your page validates, you can add the official W3C valid icons to your site.

Validate your CSS style sheets using the W3C's CSS Validator

A large site's CSS templates might get large and become difficult to test. Moreover, CSS templates can include other CSS templates. Physically checking every CSS line becomes increasingly difficult as a site's size increases. The W3C's CSS validation service automates testing your site's CSS.

1 Go to jigsaw.w3.org/css-validator.

2 Click in the Address box and type or paste the address of the page you want to validate.

3 Click 'Check'.

4 Review and correct any errors that the Validator identifies.

Remember, you cannot please everyone

You cannot please everyone. When you use the Web's latest features, ensure your webpage still functions for users with older browsers. Ensure your page is legible in all browsers, even old ones. A page does not have to be pretty, merely legible. The Web is an indispensable information source; do not exclude a group based upon disability. It is fitting this book ends with this best practice. Recall Chapter 1's mantra: provide the user with a service. You cannot create a popular service if your service only caters to a fraction of your audience. Create a website that gracefully degrades, so everyone can use your service.

1 Consider the Gumamela template at 800x600 resolution. Although not as nice as 1024x768, the page degrades and is still usable.

2 Now consider what happens when the CSS template is not applied to the page's HTML. The page, although ugly, remains legible.

Top 10 Web Design Problems Solved

Problem 1: I still don't know how to actually create a webpage. What do I do next?

Learn Hypertext Markup Language (HTML) and Cascading Style Sheets (CSS). With HTML, you use bracketed codes to tag *elements*, such as <h1> for a top-level heading, <p> for a paragraph and <img> to insert an image. Using CSS, you apply formatting to those HTML elements; for example, `h1 {font-family: arial; color: blue; }` tells the browser to display all top-level headings tagged <h1> in the Arial font and make them blue. Understanding both HTML and CSS is fundamental for creating and formatting webpages.

1 Open www.w3schools.com in your web browser. Now bookmark this site; it should become one of your most visited sites, as it is the most comprehensive resource on the Internet.

2 Notice it has tutorials and references on virtually every web-related technology, including HTML, XHTML, CSS, XML, XML DOM and JavaScript. This site has been my number one resource over the years and I trust it will become yours too.

3 Now, if you haven't already, buy a book on HTML and CSS. I recommend *HTML5 & CSS3 In Simple Steps* by Josh Hill (published by Pearson Education, 2011).

Problem 2: What do I use in HTML and CSS to create a webpage?

You have several options for creating pages in HTML and formatting them in CSS. The most basic method is to type the source code in text-only documents and then save HTML files with the .htm or .html filename extension and CSS files with the .css extension. If you are just starting out, I strongly recommend that you begin with a content management system (CMS) like WordPress. With WordPress, you can get by with very little knowledge of HTML. In addition, you can find plenty of CSS-based themes to control the layout and appearance of your site, and as you learn more about CSS you can tweak the theme. For advanced designers, I recommend high-end HTML and CSS authoring programs like Adobe's Dreamweaver or KompoZer.

1 Create and edit source code in a text editor, such as Windows Notepad or TextEdit for MacOS.

2 Use a content management system, such as WordPress, to handle most of the HTML and CSS behind the scenes.

3 Use a high-end HTML and CSS authoring program to create and format pages and then upload your files to a web server.

WHAT DOES THIS MEAN?

What You See Is What You Get (WYSIWYG): A webpage editing application where you can build a page much like you would use a program like Word or Pages. Behind the scenes, the software generates the HTML needed to represent the page you lay out visually.

HOT TIP: WYSIWYG webpage authoring programs, which include CMSs like WordPress, help you avoid HTML and CSS to some degree, but if you want to customise a site or need to troubleshoot common problems, you really need to know HTML and CSS essentials.

1

debunking-alternative.shtml - Notepad

File Edit Format View Help

`<h1>Debunking Alternative Food Allergy Tests and Therapies</h1>`

`<p><em>This article first appeared in the 2007 summer issue of Support Net, a newsletter published and distributed by <a href="http://www.kidswithfoodallergies.org/">Kids With Food Allergies</a>.</em></p>`

`<p>If you or a loved one has a <em>food allergy</em>, chances are pretty good that you have done some research on the Internet. You probably have come across some intriguing food allergy tests and treatments that your doctor failed to mention--tests and treatments with names that certainly sound legitimate, like NAET, ELISA/ACT, cytotoxic, IgG testing, and provocation-neutralization testing.</p>`

`<p>You read up on these tests and treatments, and perhaps the reasoning seems logical. Maybe your body is missing something or has too much of something that has disturbed its balance. If you just had the right vitamins and minerals, maybe you could shake that food allergy for good. So, why did your doctor fail to mention these tests and cures? Is there some medical conspiracy to keep this information under wraps?</p>`

`<p>I am a medical doctor, an allergist who specializes in diagnosing and treati...`

2

ComputerChimp.com

Manage Themes | Install Themes

Current Theme

Thesis 1.8 by Chris Pearson

A website framework so flexible and extensible that you will never have to change your theme again. Seriously. Check out the Site Options and the Design Options to begin your Thesis experience! [ver. 1.8]

OPTIONS: Widgets | Menus

Available Themes

Search Installed Themes | Feature Filter

Luxury Press 1.4 by Diamonds Designers

High Quality WordPress Theme. Green and Black. Two Column, No plugins required, Sidebar and Widget Ready. Compatible with WordPress 2.9. W3C Validated CSS & HTML. Compatible with IE and Firefox.

Styleicious 1.11 by ThaSlayer

Designed by: ThaSlayer

Activate | Preview | Delete

All of this theme's files are located in `/themes/styleicious`.

Posts, Media, Links, Pages, Comments, Thesis, Appearance, Themes, Widgets, Menus, Editor, Plugins, Users, Tools, Settings, Performance, Contact Form, Collapse menu

Howdy, Jon

3

Pearson Publishing - KompoZer

File Edit View Insert Format Table Tools Help

New Open Save Publish Browse Undo Redo Anchor Link Image Table Form CaScadeS

Body Text | (no class) | ! !!

Variable Width | B I U

Site Manager

View: All files

Name

Pearson Publishing

717px

Pearson Publishing

Home About us People History

20 ye
inno
in edu

Pearson Pu
schools, co
educationa
range of pr
using a co
fixed electr

Pearson Publishing has over 15,000 institutional

Normal | HTML Tags | Source | Preview

`<body>`

Problem 3: How do I edit photos so they look good on a webpage?

You need to learn a photo-editing tool like Adobe Photoshop Elements or GIMP. My suggestion is Adobe Photoshop Elements, as it is inexpensive, intuitive and is recommended by lots of people. Also, buy a good book that teaches you how to use the tool you select.

1 Navigate to Adobe's website where you can download a trial copy of Adobe Photoshop Elements.

HOT TIP: You can find plenty of free photo-editing and enhancement programs, including Google's Picasa and Photoscape. Such a program may be installed on your computer, as computers and printers often include photo-enhancement applications. You may also want to consider a graphics design program, such as Adobe Illustrator or CorelDraw at the higher end, Xara for something more affordable but still very capable or Inkscape (free) for drawing scalable vector images.

2 Go to amazon.co.uk and search for Adobe Photoshop Elements. There are many books, including *Adobe Photoshop Elements 10 In Simple Steps* by Joli Ballew and Ken Bluttman (published by Pearson Education, 2012).

3 If you cannot afford Adobe Photoshop Elements, then navigate to www.gimp.org and download the GNU Image Manipulation Program (GIMP).

? DID YOU KNOW?

GIMP is an open source graphics program with a long history. It is a stable, high-quality program, albeit not as easy to use as Adobe Photoshop Elements.

Problem 4: Where can I learn more about use case analysis?

There are hard references on use case analysis, and there are easy references. I recommend an easy reference, as use case analysis should not be difficult. Remember, because use cases focus on how users will use your site, it helps you make your website a service.

1 Refer back to Chapter 1, where I discuss requirements and use case analysis. This step is crucial to designing a website that meets users' needs.

2 Go to Google and search for 'use case analysis' and you will see many online references. Navigate to Wikipedia and you will find ample references.

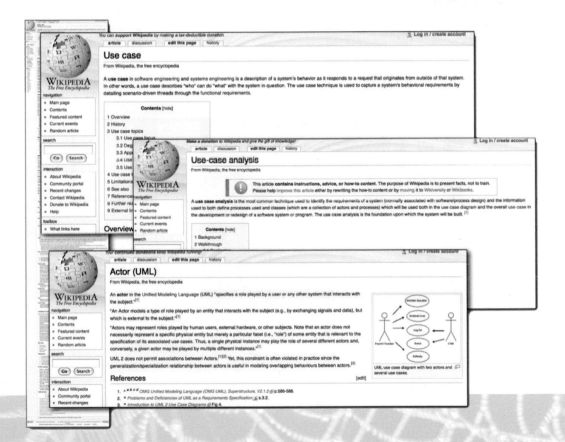

HOT TIP: Use case analysis is also used to develop rather complex systems. If you find a web reference using a complex system, keep searching – you will find a reference more applicable to web design.

3 Now navigate to the Directgov website (www.direct.gov.uk), by no means a fancy site, but a useful one.

4 Next, notice the open source Flash Site template. It is brilliant, but not very usable.

5 Now surmise which site probably conducted requirements and use case analysis. Requirements and use case analysis are important if you want to design a usable site that meets users' needs.

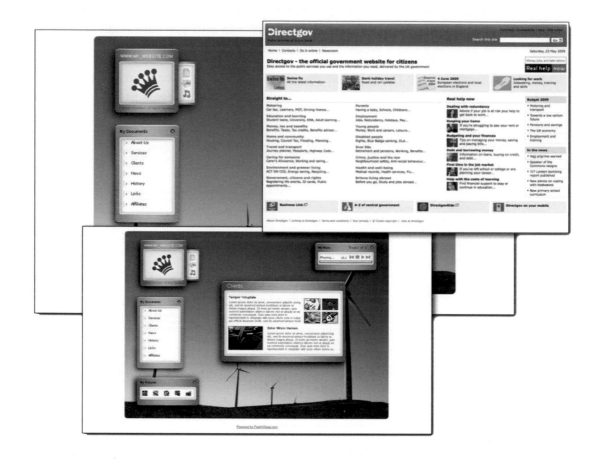

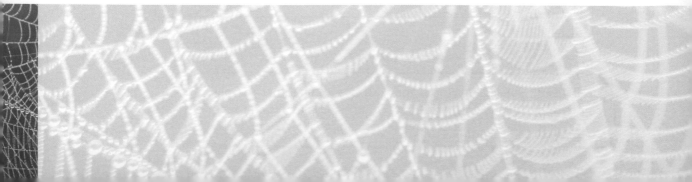

Problem 5: How do I check my work once I'm finished?

Plenty of free tools are available to assist you in checking your webpages for errors, performance, search engine optimisation, accessibility and more.

1 Check for appearance issues in the four leading web browsers: Internet Explorer, Mozilla Firefox, Google Chrome and Apple Safari.

2 Test for accessibility at fae.cita.uiuc.edu.

3 Test page load speed at developers.google.com/pagespeed.

4 Use the SeoQuake addon for Mozilla Firefox to audit your site for search engine optimisation.

5 Use W3C auditors to validate your HTML and CSS to ensure that your site conforms to web standards.

4

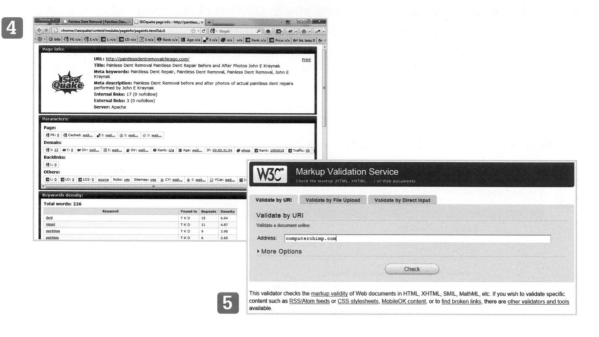

5

SEE ALSO: Chapter 10 introduces you to several free tools for checking your work, along with guidance on how to test for broken links and appearance issues in more than one web browser.

Problem 6: How do I find out if my site is achieving its goals?

Prior to initiating development, set quantifiable goals, such as the number of visitors you want on a daily basis, the average amount of time you want them to spend on your site, which pages you want them to look at most, and what you want them to do, such as sign up for a newsletter or place an order. You can then use website analytics to monitor your site for the designated activities and provide detailed reports that provide insight into how successful the site is in achieving its goals.

1 Register for a Google account and log in to your account.

2 Go to www.google.com/analytics and follow the instructions to add a tracking code to your website.

3 Return to Google Analytics after several days to evaluate the data that has been collected.

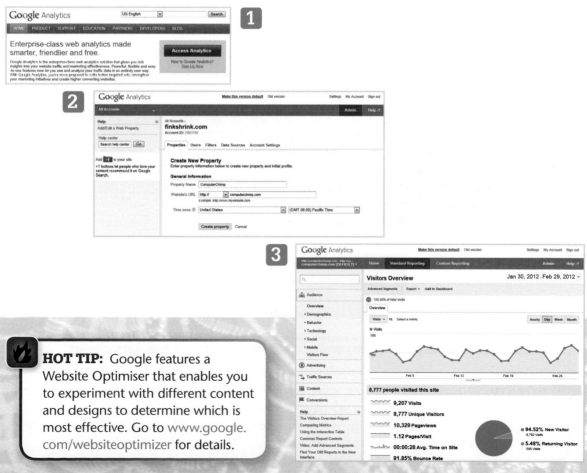

HOT TIP: Google features a Website Optimiser that enables you to experiment with different content and designs to determine which is most effective. Go to www.google. com/websiteoptimizer for details.

Problem 7: My site looks unprofessional. How do I make it appear more professional?

Consistency, accuracy and constraint; these three terms describe a website's most important features. Throughout this book I have stressed these three features. For more information you should refer back through this book.

1 Remember, your page should appear consistent. Review Chapter 2's discussion about creating headers, footers and navigation templates.

2 Remember, your pages should be accurate. Spelling and grammatical errors make your site appear unprofessional. Broken links and other page errors also make for an unprofessional website.

3 Finally, and perhaps most importantly, remember to practise restraint. Use a consistent, appealing colour palette of no more than four or five colours. Do not use images indiscriminately and do not place them haphazardly on a webpage. Instead, use a grid, and when in doubt, leave it out.

HOT TIP: Be honest with yourself. If you are not a graphic designer, admit it and seek out ways to overcome missing skills. Regardless of which CMS you use for your site, you can find plenty of professionally designed templates for less than £50. Start with a professional template and then customise it to suit your needs.

Problem 8: My website takes a long time to load. How do I fix this?

Some users might simply have bad Internet connections. But if your site loads slowly for many users, chances are there are one or more problems that cause your site's pages to load slowly. You must identify and address the causes for this behaviour.

1 Test your page speed at developers.google.com/pagespeed or other page speed test sites or by using a browser addon.

2 Address any issues that the page speed test identifies.

HOT TIP: The following are some general tips for improving website and webpage performance:

- If you are using a content management system, such as WordPress, install a plugin to cache pages, so browsers load pre-built pages instead of having to wait for the CMS to 'assemble' them.

- Use smaller images, where possible, and compress images as much as possible without overly degrading the quality.

- Minimise CSS by removing any styles that your site doesn't use. In addition, combine CSS files, so a browser needs to load fewer CSS files.

- Use CSS and text to create 'buttons' and other navigational graphics instead of images, where possible. (Text is better for SEO, too.)

- Specify image dimensions, so browsers can display a placeholder box for the image while it loads.

- Use CSS sprites to combine small images into one large image. (Search the Web for details on how to create and use CSS sprites.)

- Use HTTP expires headers to instruct browsers not to download items the browser may already have stored in its cache. (Search the Web for details on how to use HTTP expires headers.)

- Move CSS <style> tags to the beginning and JavaScript <script> tags to the end of your HTML documents where possible, so CSS styles load before the content of the page and scripts run after the page is loaded.

SEE ALSO: Chapter 10 introduces you to free web developer tools for testing the performance of a webpage and identifying issues that may be slowing it down.

Problem 9: I'm not very artistic, but can't afford to pay a web designer. What do I do?

Creating a professional, visually appealing website does not require a professional design team. With a content management system like WordPress, a free or premium template and free and royalty-free graphics, you can build an outstanding website very affordably, if not for free.

1. The easiest way to get started is to install a content management system (CMS) and a pre-designed theme or template. (Search Google for templates or themes designed specifically for the CMS you are using.)

2. Purchase royalty-free photos and other artwork for your site if you are unable to develop these yourself.

3. Instead of trying to pick your own colour scheme, let a tool like Adobe Kuler pick your palette for you.

4. Select professional looking icons from sites like www.kde-look.org and avoid cheap clip art and animated GIFs.

5. Finally, remember, eye candy is not what draws users to your site. Quality information and services attract users.

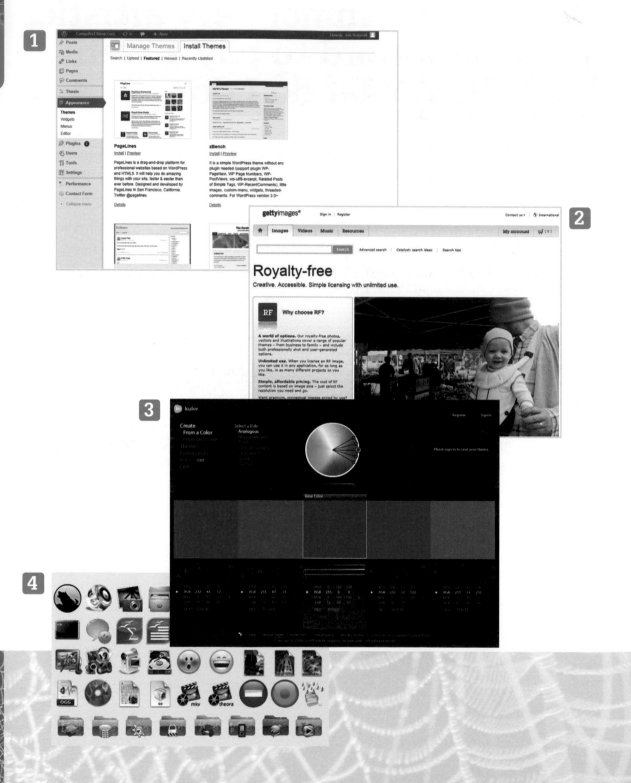

Problem 10: How do I start?

The best web designers are not always the most artistically gifted or technologically savvy. They are often the people who have the best tools and resources and know how to leverage what they have. Let the tools do most of the work as your artistic skills and technical expertise develop.

1 Open an account with a reputable hosting service.

2 Log into your account, access the control panel and install WordPress.

3 Search the Web for a theme you like and install it in WordPress.

4 Add pages and other content.

5 Explore the many features in WordPress and try to use them in a spirit of play until you become comfortable with them.

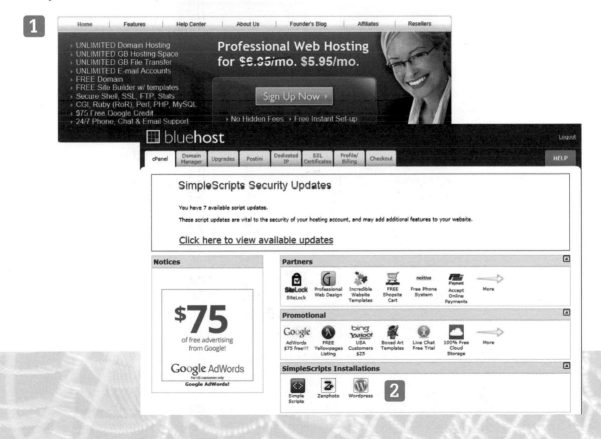

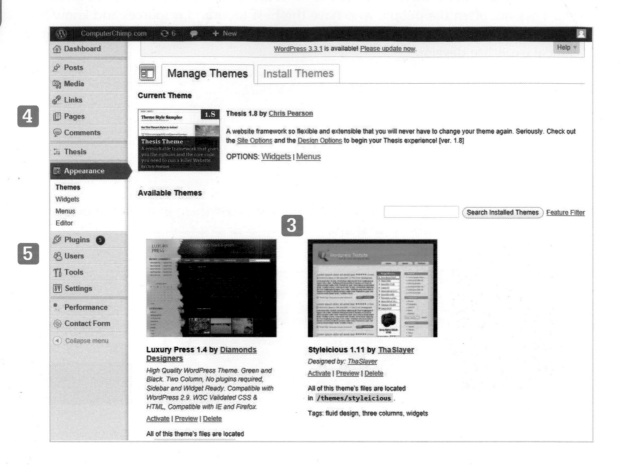

SEE ALSO: If you are just getting started and like the idea of creating and managing websites with a CMS, consider *Build Your First Website In Simple Steps* by Joe Kraynak (published by Pearson Education, 2011). This book shows how to build a website in WordPress, starting with choosing a web hosting provider.